Is it true you have two mums?

RUBY CLAY

Published by
British Association for Adoption & Fostering
(BAAF)
Saffron House
6–10 Kirby Street
London EC1N 8TS
www.baaf.org.uk

Charity registration 275689 (England & Wales)
and SC039337 (Scotland)

British Library Cataloguing in Publication Data
A catalogue record for this book is available from
the British Library

ISBN 978 1 907585 15 9

Illustration on cover by Saira Clay
Designed by Helen Joubert Design
Typeset by Fravashi Aga
Printed in Great Britain by T J International
Trade distribution by Turnaround Publisher Services, Unit 3,
Olympia Trading Estate, Coburg Road, London N22 6TZ

BAAF is the leading UK-wide membership organisation for all
those concerned with adoption, fostering and child care issues.

The paper used in this book is FSC certified.
FSC (The Forest Stewardship Council) is an international network
to promote responsible management of the world's forests.

Printed on chlorine-free paper

Contents

Acknowledgements

My thanks go first and foremost to my partner, Gail, for her unfailing support, honest feedback and essential supplies of tea and cake through long hours writing into the night. Thanks also to our wonderful dynamic daughters for being themselves, for making this book what it is and for sharing their thoughts with me so generously. I would like to thank our first social worker, Barbara, who believed in us and fought for us against the tide of public and professional opinion at the time, and my thanks go to all the dear friends who have stood by us as a family through joyful and challenging times. I would like to pay tribute to our tenacious fellow travellers on the adoption journey in the Northern Support Group, and particularly to Chris, whose conversation and writing has often inspired and affirmed my own.

My thanks go also to the editor of this book, Hedi Argent, for her gentle encouragement and wisdom; to Sarah Borthwick and Brenda Stones for reading and commenting on the script; and to Shaila Shah and Jo Francis for managing the publication. Lastly, I would like to thank my father, who I hope will find this a good read, and my mother who, sadly, died without seeing it completed and to whom I owe so much.

All names have been changed, including my own, in order to protect the privacy of my daughters.

About the author

Ruby Clay is an Asian lesbian trainer and writer, who lives in the north of England with her partner, her three daughters and her elderly father. She enjoys hill-walking and writing fiction, and travels with her family to Scotland on a regular basis and to India whenever she can.

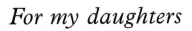
For my daughters

The Our Story series
This book is part of BAAF's Our Story series, which explores adoption and fostering experiences as told by adoptive parents and foster carers.

Also available in the series:

The series editor
Hedi Argent is an independent family placement consultant, trainer and freelance writer. She is the author of *Find me a Family* (Souvenir Press, 1984), *Whatever Happened to Adam?* (BAAF, 1998), *Related by Adoption* (BAAF, 2004), *One of the Family* (BAAF, 2005), *Ten Top Tips for Placing Children in Permanent Families* (BAAF, 2006), *Josh and Jaz have Three Mums* (BAAF, 2007), *Ten Top Tips for Placing Siblings* (BAAF, 2008), and *Ten Top Tips for Supporting Kinship Placements* (BAAF, 2009). She is the co-author of *Taking Extra Care* (BAAF, 1997, with Ailee Kerrane) and *Dealing with Disruption* (BAAF, 2006, with Jeffrey Coleman), and the editor of *Keeping the Doors Open* (BAAF, 1988), *See You Soon* (BAAF, 1995), *Staying Connected* (BAAF, 2002), and *Models of Adoption Support* (BAAF, 2003). She has also written six illustrated booklets in the children's series published by BAAF: *What Happens in Court?* (2003, with Mary Lane), *What is Contact?* (2004), *What is a Disability?* (2004), *Life Story Work* (2005, with Shaila Shah), *What is Kinship Care?* (2007) and *Adopting a Brother or Sister* (2010).

1

Introducing us

This is my take on the last eighteen years' experience of becoming and being an adoptive parent. If my partner, Gail, were to write it, or any of our three daughters, I imagine it would turn out quite a different story. The possibilities of reaching an objective viewpoint in a family seem seriously limited to me; it all depends on which side of the kitchen table you sit. I have drawn heavily for the earlier chapters on interviews a friend of ours conducted with us in 1995. These reveal how quickly history rewrites itself in the minds of those living it. There were points even then when Gail and I had different recollections of some detail of a conversation a year before. Returning to those interview transcripts now, I can see how much has altered in my memory in the intervening decade and a half. What follows is a very partial and subjective snapshot of the creation of a family through adoption.

Gail and I have been together for over twenty years. We have been approved as adopters both by our home local authority and, at a later stage, by another adoption agency, and once went part-way through a fostering assessment. We adopted three children, not birth siblings, separately over a period of six years. Maya, who was eight when she was placed with us, is now twenty-four and as much part of the family as she always has been, although she's living independently three hundred miles away. Lubna, who arrived as a diminutive sixteen-month-old to turn our lives upside down, is now a cool fourteen; and Saira, who was only seven months old when we carried her into our home, is already ten and poised to leave primary school; we are at that point of mourning when we will finally leave our afternoons at the school gate behind forever. It would appear that we are veterans of the adoption process, and certainly we know a thing or two about our own daughters, about each other and about ourselves after all these years of intense family life and, before that, the years of intense waiting for family life. Yet the longer I go on, the more I realise the extent of my ignorance and naivety. I write this today not from a position of experience or wisdom or competence, but from a place of humility and incredulity that it ever came to pass that I became that most loaded of titles, a mother, and not just a mother but one of two mothers, a co-mother, one half of a mothering partnership.

There are many things to say by way of introduction, and many ways of introducing our family. The most relevant, initially, may be that Gail and I are lesbians and our children are all girls. Having two mothers is a significant fact about our children's lives. A close second is that we are all Asian except Gail, who is white with some Irish heritage. Maya and I both have Indian parents and some Scottish and Irish as well as Indian heritage in earlier generations of our families. My parents migrated to Britain as young adults in 1949, and Maya's birth mother also came to Britain as an adult in the 1980s. Maya's birth father has never left India. Lubna and Saira are both of dual white and British-born Pakistani heritage. Being black is much talked about in our family and plays a big part in our children's friendships and networks outside the home.

Also significant for our identity as a family is the fact that our middle daughter is deaf and has some learning difficulties. Being adoptive parents is significant to Gail and me because how we have made our family is part of our identity as parents. The significance of being adopted seems to wax and wane for the children as they grow and may be different for each of them at different points in their lives.

All these are not just statistics for the 2011 census: they are pertinent facts that deeply affect the minutiae of daily life in our house, like the fact that we live in the heart of an Asian community in a northern city that has lost its industries; or the fact that, as a couple, we are university-educated and middle-class. More importantly, Gail and the children and I are not the sum of our household. Since just before Saira was placed, we have had my parents living with us in true extended family style. They live in the ground floor rooms and we live upstairs, accessing our garden through my parents' dining room. Having other adults in the house was hugely important to Maya when she was a teenager and she has a particularly close relationship with them. We have all been influenced by the stream of idiosyncratic older relatives visiting my parents through the years with their greying hair and brown skins, their Anglo-Indian ways and their reminiscences of Indian childhoods, like the stories that wafted through my own childhood and seeped into my pores.

So, how to begin to sum up our last eighteen years' experience of adoption? And why does it matter? Well, I suppose it matters because some people – thousands, if not millions of people possibly – think that we shouldn't have been allowed to adopt Maya, Lubna and Saira in the first place, and condemn our children's home life as unnatural and immoral. It might also matter because some people – many people – think it's irrelevant that six out of seven members of our household are Asian and that our children find their Asian heritage reflected in mine. It matters because people will say, when the prospect of lesbians and gay men adopting is raised, that this is an added burden for an already disadvantaged child to take on. Does that sound too political? Well, the Family as an institution is deeply political in all its many manifestations and our family seems to accommodate all manner of thorny political debates quite comfortably within the fabric of our individual and collective lives.

Gail and I met as teachers of English as a Second Language working in the same inner city comprehensive, teaching children who had recently migrated to Britain from poor rural backgrounds in Pakistan and Bangladesh, had fled civil war in Somalia, or whose parents had come to Britain to study from countries like South Korea and Libya. Gail and I recognised each other as lesbians in a climate when it was not safe to be out as a lesbian teacher, even to other staff. We watched each others' backs in the professional and emotional battlefield that is a large secondary school, and we also looked out for the students we taught, who had no power or voice in the school's community and were often reeling from the culture shock of arriving in Britain, and from devastating experiences of loss, dislocation, bereavement and violent conflict.

During these years of friendship that preceded our relationship as partners, we learnt to read each other and depend on each other. In an environment of intense and bitter political conflict around multicultural and anti-racist education, national teachers' strikes, and the implementation of Clause 28 of the Local Government Act, which made "promoting homosexuality" in schools a crime, we discovered that we shared the same instincts and we felt seen and understood by each other in our responses to crises. The trust and solidarity of those early years of campaigning have stood us in good stead as prospective adopters and as adoptive parents.

Gail had trained as a teacher of English as a Foreign Language with the intention of eventually teaching abroad in Central or South America, as she speaks fluent Spanish. With time, she found that what she had wanted from going to Nicaragua could just as easily be achieved in the UK, but she still wanted to do something bigger and more meaningful with her life; going to work each day and living for the school holidays was not enough for her. I was searching similarly for a fulfilling and inspiring direction for myself. Contributing something to society may sound corny or trite in a post-feminist world in which there is, famously, "no such thing as society", but Gail and I both grew up in strong Labour Party households. For us, contributing to the greater collective good was core to our motivation and self-esteem.

And we were restless.

2

In the beginning

Gail and I sit by the gently crackling fire in our mulberry-carpeted front room. Faded Indian hangings clothe the walls and we lift our mugs of milky coffee from a low wood and brass table on stumpy carved legs. It is an adult room with lethal brass poker and tongs left casually on the hearth, a video machine gaping open-mouthed at floor level beneath the small television, and piles of important papers and bills in transit on the floor awaiting attention beside each of our accustomed seats. The house is built into a steep hill so that the front is one storey above the road, and the front door, opening directly into this room in a peculiarly Yorkshire fashion, is reached by steep, uneven, impossibly inaccessible stone steps outside. At this elevation, we can leave the pink velvet curtains in the bay window open onto the winter's night to reveal a view that plunges down a black tunnel of back gardens and reaches across the whole valley's breadth of quivering orange street lights to meet the matching blank void of unlit parkland on the opposite hillside. It is a view and a scene to warm the heart, but our hearts are not warm – they are puzzled and fidgety and inexplicably dissatisfied.

We are both wondering, what now?

We have toyed with ideas of working in India and South America at various times. It might seem that we have everything we could wish for: a stable, loving relationship, a comfortable income, interesting and satisfying jobs, a home we have invested a lot of time and effort in putting our own stamp on, and serious creative interests to occupy our leisure time. Gail is busy developing herself as an artist, and I have a published teenage novel just about to hit the bookshops, or more likely the bottom shelves of a few school libraries.

I examine our life as I watch fluid orange flames snake over the glowing coals in front of me. I left teaching in the school where we met some time back and now work part-time as a refuge worker in a local Asian women's refuge. In addition to supporting women in fear and distress, fleeing violent partners, this involves spending a lot of time unblocking drains, moving furniture, fixing curtain rails that bored children have swung from, and sundry other unsavoury tasks that I hadn't signed up for and don't feel skilled in. One unanticipated role thrust upon me in this post has a quite revelatory effect when it happens, and that is holding babies. Because I am a teacher, it is assumed I know everything there is to know about children of any age and I am regularly left in charge of anyone under the age of sixteen, while women residents attend urgent appointments with other staff. Some of these young people touch me deeply and I remember them still nearly twenty years later.

'Look, she likes you,' someone says as I sit in the office, a baby perched gingerly on my knee and looking up at me with large dark eyes of such profound seriousness that I am transfixed. 'You'd make a good mother.' I laugh it off, but feel secretly pleased and I am convinced this baby and I understand each other and are communicating in some universal language of the eyes. A year later, when I visit her in the bleak fifth storey flat her mother has been re-housed in, and she has learnt to walk and throw things and scream 'No' in Punjabi, I realise there is a vast amount more to this than looking into each other's eyes. But a seed has been sown.

And there is already another seed pushing a shoot of an idea up through the dense, sluggish soil of my subconscious. Two years ago, an Asian lesbian friend of mine applied to adopt. At that time, no lesbian adopter or foster carer approved by our local authority had ever "come out" in the assessment process so, although she was in a relationship, she applied as a single adopter. Her partner moved out of their house while my friend was being approved and was only brought into the assessment briefly in the guise of a potential childminder. I was deeply uneasy about the deception involved, but the idea that I could adopt fixed itself somewhere in my consciousness as a future option waiting to surface at an appropriate time. It seemed that time was now.

'What about adopting?' I volunteer lightly, in a "just-an-idea" sort of way, staring carefully into the fire.

'Would you want to? Really?' Gail is excited. 'I think it's a great idea. We'd be good parents, wouldn't we? And they'd snap you up. Look at how quickly Sita moved in with Tanya and Ros. They're always saying they haven't got enough black and Asian adopters.' She pauses. 'I don't want to do it like they did, though, moving Ros out of the house and pretending she was just the childminder or something. They got themselves in such a mess, like the social worker would come to the house and she'd be there in the bath, or hoovering or something, and she was just meant to be this, like, "friend". And they were so worried Sita would let the cat out of the bag. It's not fair on the child.'

We sit quietly trying to think our way around the reality of our life together. There is no hiding it. There is no wanting to hide it. Why would we? Why would we want to hide a good, solid, nurturing partnership? We are proud of ourselves, and what we have to offer, and we want to shout about it. Denying who we are is unthinkable to us. Looking back, I can see I was quite naïve and privileged as a middle-class professional lesbian with a heterosexual past. I had little idea of the odds still stacked against us in the last decade of the twentieth century. Except to other lesbians, my sexual orientation was mostly invisible behind my plait of thick dark hair, my sallow winter skin and the Indian *salwar khameez* I often wore at home and at work; the conjunction of "Asian" and "lesbian" being a contradiction in terms to most people. At that point I had little experience of unfettered homophobia.

'No, we'd have to be out,' I agree. 'It's the only way to do it. And also if we get through, then that would be much better for other women who might think about it in the future...We've got loads in our favour: we're middle class, we're trained teachers with bags of childcare experience, and we know they need more black adopters. If we get through, then other lesbians might get through further down the line...' Already India and South America have faded into oblivion beside the living, breathing concrete reality that has walked confidently into the room. This is what we want to do with our carefully crafted life: we want to share it. We want to open it up to all the turmoil and challenge and glorious messiness of having children. We want other complicated, assertive, wilful human beings to poke sticky fingers into the video slot and scrawl beaming bodiless faces with legs and arms sticking out at odd angles on the vitally important bills. We will settle for nothing less out of life.

'How on earth do we start, though?' Gail frowns anxiously. 'I mean, we can't just ring up and say, "We're a lesbian couple and we want to adopt a child", can we? They might say we're not allowed. And someone in the department might know us, in fact they're almost bound to know you, everyone knows you.' It's true. In an earlier incarnation as a school/community liaison teacher, building links between my secondary school and local black parents and communities, I made it my business to be known quite widely in education and community work circles across the city. I'm starting to regret having been so good at it already. 'It could get all round the city in no time, you know what a village this is when it comes to gossip. What if it got back to the new head?' Gail has not got the measure of this latest in a long line of changing head teachers, and a new boss is always a danger for any lesbian or gay teacher. Something comes back to me from sitting on a bus earlier in the week.

'When I was coming back from town on Saturday, I saw a council advert,' I interrupt. 'It showed some different children's faces, black and white, and it said something like, "Could you care for a child like this? Could you foster or adopt? You don't have to be married, you don't have to be white, you don't have to have a garden..." It sounded quite welcoming and like they really want different kinds of adopters. What if I rang up and said, "I've seen the advert and I'm an Asian woman and I'm interested in adopting?" Then when I've sussed it all out and got more of an idea of who we're dealing with and whether it's safe, we could tell them about you.'

'That feels better,' Gail nods.

'So we're agreed then? We're going to do it?'

'Wow!'

'Scary!'

'Exciting.'

Silence as neurons whizz around brain cells.

'And we're thinking of Asian children, right?'

'Oh yes! I mean, I think so. I don't want to be the only black person in a white family. But what about you? What if you felt left out?'

'Why on earth would I feel left out? I'm surrounded by white people wherever I look. We live in my world, don't we?'

More silence as I try to think of more angles on this. It occurs to me that we might have started at the wrong end of this conversation. Our starting point has been that of wanting to adopt. We haven't considered other ways of having children.

'Would you rather get pregnant?'

'No way! I mean, I'd love to have children but I can't see the attraction of being pregnant or giving birth; all that pain and feeling sick and having doctors poking around inside you.' Gail makes a face. 'I hate this assumption that all women want to give birth. I just think that's fiction, you know. I used to think I'd get to this age when suddenly I'd have this burning urge to give birth, but it hasn't happened so far and I don't think it ever will. The other thing I don't like about it is this idea that you want to reproduce your genes, that idea of leaving a little bit of "me" behind, I just think that's rubbish. And everybody would assume that there's a man in the picture, or that there was a man for one night at least, and it affects how people think about you. You've got to deal with all these professional people, like doctors, where you've either got to play out some charade or you've got to keep justifying and explaining what you're doing... And the other thing is that there are all these kids in care needing parents, so why would we want to go and produce another one?'

'That's good!' I laugh when she draws breath, 'Because I don't fancy it either, and anyway I can't imagine how we'd deal with getting a donor...'

I run through the options in my head: we don't really know anyone who could be a donor – it's not an easy thing to ask. And I wouldn't want to go for an anonymous donor through a clinic. It's taken me long enough to sort out my identity as an Asian woman when I've grown up with my Asian parents. I hate the idea of bringing a child into the world who won't know who their father is. Maybe it's OK for white children, I'm not even sure about that, but for black children, I think they need to know all the specifics they can get hold of to have a positive identity: language, religion, even things like the exact village their ancestors came from. I know you can't always have all that and lots of children never get to know anything about their fathers, but what happens by accident and circumstance is different from setting out to deprive a child of half their heritage.

'This isn't about having babies, is it? It's about wanting to adopt. That's different,' I say.

I'm glad we have sorted that one out and, as often happens, have found that we're pointing in the same direction even before we've checked out whether we're on the same road. I sense it's important to pause at every step and check for wrong assumptions and missed feelings. This is major construction work and if we don't clear the ground properly first, our foundations will not be safe.

Eighteen years later, I can say we did as good a job of clearing the ground as we were capable of at the time, but at just turned thirty, neither of us could know all that lay in our own histories and psyches to trip us up further down the line. We presented as hugely experienced and dazzlingly competent and no one, including ourselves, was aware of how much we still didn't know about what we were taking on, where our individual vulnerabilities would be, and where the vulnerabilities would be in our partnership. And for us, partnership is everything. It was always our intention to be equally involved as two very active mothers. Harmony of parenting styles, effective communication and shared understanding were necessary and crucial from the beginning.

3

Getting started

Initially I rang anonymously and made a general enquiry about whether our local authority adoption section would ever consider a lesbian applicant to adopt. The person who took the call was friendly and straightforward. She said the department did not discriminate on any grounds and assessed all applicants purely on their abilities to parent children who had had difficult experiences. We felt we knew about helping children who had experienced neglect, abuse and loss from our work in inner-city schools, and my work in the women's refuge. It was as if someone had pushed a door slightly open for us but we were a long way from being able to walk through.

We didn't feel we should be "out" as a couple before the agency even knew us. As far as we could tell, gay couples had never been out to the department before, despite several lesbian foster carers and adoptive parents having been approved by the agency in the past as single carers. I was particularly nervous as I was a council employee myself, seconded to the women's refuge from social services. Personnel files on me were held in the same building as the adoption department, so it felt too risky for us to just bounce in there and say, 'We're lesbians and we want to adopt!' The next time I approached the adoption section, I introduced myself as an Asian woman on my own wanting to adopt, and gave them my name. The manager asked me in for a chat and was very pleasant and helpful but there was no way I had any intention of coming out to her. Our friend Tanya, who had been through the whole thing as a single adopter, had warned me that this manager had strong Christian views and I didn't trust how she would respond to a family of two mothers.

The other thing Tanya had told us was how, as a single black adopter, she was sent on a preparation course with a roomful of white heterosexual couples and it was a nightmare. When it became apparent that there were no white babies but a lot of very young black children needing placements, the white couples laid into the social workers about why they couldn't have a black baby and it was very upsetting for Tanya, who had really struggled with her identity growing up with a white mum. So I said I was a bit worried about the training, being a single woman and being black, and the manager told me they had other single black adopters coming forward and they were going to put on a separate course for us.

There were only three of us, and it was both a luxury and quite exposing and challenging to have such exclusive attention from the social workers running the course. That was the only stage of the process during which either of us had to deceive, and it was uncomfortable for me having to think on my feet and remember I was supposed to be single when they asked us to share examples from our own lives and personal circumstances. Most of the course content was material I was familiar with as a teacher and refuge worker. At least one of the other women on the course also had a background in childcare and early years education, so we were able to tackle the tasks with some confidence. After each session I went through all the exercises and handouts with Gail at home.

We also started talking to some of our friends about what we were doing and tried to find out more about the adoption agency. After Tanya's experience, we felt we needed a social worker who wasn't going to have problems with us being lesbians. We knew a fostering worker called Liz who was a lesbian, and she told us that, of all the people in the adoption section, she felt a new black social worker called Barbara was the most likely to be OK. She was out to Barbara herself and Barbara was fine with her...so we started to think about how we could make sure we got Barbara as our social worker.

At the end of the preparation course, participants were asked to go away and think about whether they still felt adoption was for them and to write to the department if the answer was yes. I wrote straight away and said I wanted to go ahead and that I would feel more comfortable dealing with all the issues about identity in the assessment if I could have a black social worker (knowing Barbara was the only one!). Although, in retrospect, my writing as a supposedly single black adopter saying, 'I want a black social worker', feels a little unfair on Barbara, and gave her no idea of what she might be letting herself in for, we felt justified in protecting ourselves at that point because we really didn't know whom we could trust. It was also important and true that perceptions of racial identity were going to be a huge issue in the assessment, and in finding children. Having a social worker who was comfortable talking about ethnic origin would have been our first issue if we had been a heterosexual couple. As a lesbian couple at that time, we were more focused on finding a social worker who wasn't homophobic, and so we felt very lucky that the two happened to come together in the person of Barbara!

I suspect my letter caused a stir in the adoption department. We got the impression that you weren't supposed to choose which social worker you were allocated, so our request felt like a huge risk. We were quite scared of alienating the agency before we began, and I worried that the white social workers who had delivered the training course would feel I was criticising their handling of ethnicity issues on the course. Whatever happened behind the scenes, the next we knew was when Barbara phoned me to introduce herself as my social worker and to arrange a visit.

Gail and I decided that I would meet her alone on the first occasion, as we didn't want her to just walk in and be confronted with the two of us. Before she came, we went round the house trying to look at our home through the eyes of a social worker, leaving a certain amount of lived-in, child-friendly clutter lying around, without it looking a complete tip. We didn't worry about putting things away, like removing lesbian books from our shelves, but we did consciously display the children's books we had. Children came in and out of the house a lot anyway, so we had thought about what was OK to have around before. We did take one picture down – a print of a classic Indian miniature hanging at the top of the stairs. In a lot of Indian miniature paintings women's upper bodies are uncovered, which wouldn't normally have been controversial, but we started to worry about assumptions Barbara might make: did Gail, as a white woman, objectify black women as exotic? Once we had voiced it, we couldn't walk past it without feeling anxious about how it would be seen, so in the end we thought, let's not have that at the top of the stairs, just put it somewhere else. It wasn't that we didn't want anyone to see it, but we feared she wouldn't see it with our eyes, and could possibly interpret something from it that we would have no control over.

Barbara's first visit was every bit as nerve-wracking as coming out to my parents, and oddly similar as Barbara, younger than us by nearly a decade, was going to be our substitute "elder" for the next two years: assessing our readiness, promoting us to other elders, and brokering a match for us with our future children in a very publicly scrutinised arrangement of parenting every bit as delicate as the arrangement of a marriage. She burst into our lives and our living room in a whirlwind of optimism and youthful energy, her wide, laughing smile brooking no opposition and the sparkling eyes in her sharp-featured ebony face flashing understanding and warmth.

As she settled down with the drink I had made her, a small poised figure balanced on the edge of the settee, I took a deep breath. She looked so relaxed and unconcerned. For her, this was routine. So far. She took a large sheaf of papers out of her bag.

'Now, there are a few things I need to run through before we get started, if I can just find the right form.' She began shuffling through her papers.

'Actually, Barbara...' She looked up, hearing something unusual in my voice. 'There's something I haven't told you...'

4

You're doing what?

Friends

Reactions from friends to our plan to adopt were varied and colourful. Some focused on the challenge of caring for children with difficult experiences, others on the risk of being out at a time when very few "out" lesbians or gay men had ever been approved. Several of our friends thought we were brave being out, a few thought us naïve, and some thought we were being deliberately "political", taking on the system rather than focusing on having a child in a less publicly contested way.

Tanya and Ros: 'You're crazy. There's no way anybody can ever get through whilst being out: take it from us, we've done this. The system is totally against women like us and you have to use every trick in the book to get round it any way you can. If you really wanted a child you'd lie, it's the only way to guarantee it...What you're doing, you risk losing everything. And once they know about you in one authority, you can't go to another and hide. If it goes wrong, that's it, your cover's blown everywhere.'

Gail: 'But if we have to pretend we're not lesbians then: one, that really hurts, pretending I'm something I'm not because someone says who I am is a bad thing to be; and two, what sort of basis would that be for a child, having to hide something about their home life? And what happens when some neighbour, or somebody at school who really hates you, rings up social services and says, "We've got this child at our school living with a lesbian couple, what are you going to do about it?"'

Ros: 'It's too late by then. The child's yours. And you know how stretched they are. If they took every child into care whose nosy neighbour reported the parents, there'd be no families left in one piece in the country.'

Me, dubious: 'But if they've known all along, they can just say to the nosy neighbour, "Yeah, we know. Your point is?" If they haven't known, and you're outed by some crackpot, then what? Wouldn't we be looking over our shoulders all the time, worried someone was going to take her back?'

Tanya is getting angry: 'Just let them try! Now we've got Sita, no one's going to take her away from us.'

Me: 'I hate doing anything underhand. Apart from anything else, we're crap liars! And the practicalities of it, you know, implicating your referees and your family. I don't like the thought of being so deliberately deceptive when mostly we're not. We don't usually have to hide our sexuality – we're just kind of selective with the truth, depending on the circumstances. It feels…well, wrong…' My voice trails away.

Ros is patient and continues as if explaining to a child in words of one syllable: 'But you're *only* lying because *they're* wrong. If the world was fair and lesbians weren't oppressed, you wouldn't have to hide who you are. You don't owe those homophobes in the council anything. There's some child out there, like Sita, who really needs you two. Are you seriously going to risk taking yourselves out of that child's life for the sake of telling the truth to people you don't even know, who couldn't care less about you?'

Me: 'Yes.' Ros throws her hands up in despair.

Liz, a lesbian social worker: 'I can understand why you're doing it this way, being out and all, but you'll never get through. Or you might get approved, but dream on if you think you're ever going to get a child placed with you. I work in Children and Families myself and I know what some of these people are like, the managers…and the panel members, honestly, you should see the panel members! I'm really worried about you putting yourselves through this…'

Rukhsana, who came to our city with four young children, fleeing domestic violence before the refuge was set up, and now job-shares a refuge worker post with me: 'You and Gail will be wonderful parents. You are guardians to my children in my will. You've always been here for my family. Now let me help you. I don't understand how this adoption works, but if there's anything I can do, just ask me.' We ask her to be our referee.

Carol, who is also being assessed, but not as a lesbian, is nervous that our outing of ourselves might bring her under scrutiny: 'You're not really interested in children, you're just interested in the cause…I don't believe you can want to adopt that much or you wouldn't take the risk of coming out.'

Various incredulous lesbians: 'Why aren't you going for artificial insemination? We're so lucky to have a local clinic happy to help us with no questions asked. Why would you want to do anything else with that on your doorstep? It's so much easier.'

Various incredulous Asian women: 'Why are they doing all these tests and interviews? They should be so grateful to have you!'

Sharon and Sarah: 'We think it's a really good idea. Go for it, we're right behind you!' And they were. A few years later they were approved as a couple to foster adolescents. Their second placement, a girl with moderate learning difficulties, was with them from the age of eleven and is still part of their family at the age of twenty-three, having long ago left the care system.

Families

Gail and I took similar paths to coming out as lesbians long before we even knew each other. We both grew up assuming ourselves to be heterosexual and discounting early passionate feelings about women because we had no language or context in which to make sense of them. We had relationships with men for a while and went on to discover relationships with women in our early twenties, at a time when being a lesbian was sometimes seen as a political choice for radical feminists. Women were organising politically and emotionally, around peace and resistance to domestic and sexual violence, at Greenham Common Women's Peace Camp, in Reclaim the Night marches and in local women's groups, usually spearheaded by lesbians, to set up refuges across the country for heterosexual women fleeing male violence.

We shared similar, largely positive, experiences of coming out to our families, who took our announcements, and later our partners, in their stride after a little temporary dismay and embarrassment. Gail comes from a large, boisterous family of five siblings who mostly live in one town in Essex within a couple of miles of the house they all grew up in. She felt a need in her teens to leave home and establish her own identity and came north to go to university. When she came out as a lesbian, her parents and her siblings were accepting and unsurprised. They embraced her subsequent partners and welcomed me into the kindly scrum of their chaotic family gatherings with affection and undemonstrative ease. They have been solidly behind us throughout the adoptions and maintain regular contact with us, despite the two hundred miles that separate us. The deaths of Gail's parents and other difficult family events have only served to bring us all closer together.

21

Gail's father, George, had been a slightly remote and autocratic figure in her childhood, a head teacher who commuted to work and was often absent in her waking hours as a young child. He mellowed after retirement and a stroke, and by the time I knew him he was a gruff, jovial grandfather with an expression of slight bewilderment and a passion for conversations about his beloved home county of Yorkshire, in which he saw me as an ally, having lived all my life in said county! He was unequivocally warm and accepting of me as Gail's partner and was positive about our chosen paths insofar as he could grasp them as he became more frail and confused. In later years, a long-buried playfulness would erupt in him, prompted by the arrival of Lubna and Saira. His eyes would dance with amusement as Lubna lectured him about wearing his hearing aids and demonstrated her own, while toddler Saira quietly accosted him with soft toys. They remember him with great affection.

While Gail's father suffered a long, slow decline, Gail's mother, Mary, was a force to be reckoned with to the end of her life, an intelligent, exotic and fearless woman of strong opinions and maverick habits, whose life was an uneasy struggle between conformity to the expectations of her times and an original, creative self-expression that never really found its voice, but is somehow honoured posthumously in the flowering of Gail's own career as an artist. Her first response to Gail's announcement on the telephone that we were thinking of adopting was characteristically left-field:

'What? A child?'

'Well, not a humpbacked whale.'

'Why do you want to complicate your lives? I thought you were both so happy?'

'We are, and we want to adopt.'

'Well, I must say I don't think they'll let you. You haven't got a garden.'

'I think not having a garden is the least of our problems. We'll just have to convince them, won't we?'

Her responses often missed the mark with Gail, as ours do with our daughters, the power of parents to disappoint being universal and unavoidable, but on the whole Mary did a sterling job of hanging in there with us through the tough times and delighting in our children when they arrived, despite already having ten grandchildren when Maya joined the family. At the regular Essex gatherings of her five children and partners, her grandchildren, and eventually great-grandchildren, all crammed impossibly into a small suburban semi, Mary would catch one or other of our children at some point in the general melée and pay them a little treasured attention to show how she was keeping tabs on their activities. The experience of a large, noisy family, with its endless possibilities of connection and allegiance, in which you sometimes have to shout to be heard and assert yourself to be fed, has been a healthy contrast for our children to the more hushed and polite afternoon tea table we share most days with my parents and their visitors.

It was always going to be crucial how my parents responded to our adoption plans. When we started out on our quest, we lived a ten-minute drive from them and saw them most weekends for a couple of hours, so we knew they were going to be significant figures in our children's lives. We didn't know then that we would make the radical decision to sell both houses and move in together some years later when my father was diagnosed with Parkinson's disease. Since Maya was thirteen and Lubna was three, we have all shared a rambling end-of-terrace house that unfolds upwards and outwards like a Tardis, and their role in our family life has been more central than ever.

I came out to my parents when I started my first relationship with a woman at the age of twenty-five. I told my mother in a classic "I've-got-something-to-tell-you" moment (of which there had already been a few in my young adulthood) in a department store café. Her first emotion was relief, as she was anticipating, ironically, the far greater crisis, in her eyes, of a pregnancy outside a committed relationship. Her second response was to tell me that her own eldest, and favourite, sister, who died before I was born, had had a number of "girlfriends" in her youth, scandalising the neighbourhood in downtown Calcutta, before an unhappy marriage and an early death. She wanted me to understand that I was telling her nothing new or beyond her experience and her support was to be taken as read from the start. I was particularly moved, and spooked, to discover I had been carrying this sister's name as my middle name all my life without knowing her story.

My father was more unsettled by my disclosure and I had to reassure him that it was not personal and he hadn't failed in any way as a father. His more sensible anxiety that I would suffer discrimination in my career seemed entirely reasonable to me at a time when homophobia against lesbian and gay teachers was rife and not illegal. He understood that I would not be intimidated out of being myself by anyone and he was proud of me for that, as it fitted very much with his own values.

By the time Gail and I decided to adopt, my parents and younger sister, who is my only sibling, had long accepted Gail into the family. They greeted our announcement with the mixed feelings of supportive trepidation with which they tended to greet all my Big Plans. In contrast to Gail's parents, my parents had no grandchildren when we started on the adoption trail so they were excited about the prospect, while a little nervous of how challenging the children might be and what kind of a rollercoaster ride I intended taking them on. My father thought it was good that we were going to be out because he is absolutely obsessed with being honest. At the same time, he was worried about how homophobic society is and concerned that we might face a lot of hurt and disappointment. It was hard for them to see the struggle we had at times during the process.

By the time we were finally matched with our first child, my sister and her husband were well advanced on the road to having a child themselves. Maya and Heather arrived in our families within weeks of each other: Maya as a fully-formed eight-year-old, complete with long, dark pony-tail bobbing on her back; and Heather, her cousin, as a newborn baby with a few thin wisps of blond hair from her father, and almond-shaped brown eyes testifying to her mother's Indian heritage. My parents lavished equal attention on both and have never differentiated between their three adopted and two birth grandchildren. My sister and her family live about forty miles away and we used to see them every few weeks, less so now the children are older and so much busier with their various hobbies and sporting activities at the weekends. The four younger children are all quite close in age: there is just a year between Heather and Lubna, and only a few weeks between Thomas and Saira.

Living with my parents over the last eleven years has meant our children have grown up comfortable and confident with adults of all generations. It also means they have had a different experience of me than they might otherwise have had, because they have seen me interacting with my own parents on a daily basis. I find it impossible to judge how helpful, or not, this has been! I imagine there's a lot of learning about relationships for children in multi-generational households like ours. Both my parents confide in Maya quite a lot now she is an adult, and find her a great comfort and support in their struggles with illness and old age. Clearing out the rabbits with her grandfather one day, Lubna observed, 'You and me, Grandpa, we make a good team.'

5

Plain sailing

'Oh-kay.' Barbara takes a deep breath and gives me a wry sideways smile. 'Ruby Clay, what are you trying to do to me?'

'I'm sorry. I know I should have said something before, but we really wanted to know who we were coming out to first – you know?' I scan her face hopefully for signs that she is on our side.

'I suppose I can understand that. And I'd like you to feel that you can trust me.' She pauses as if wondering how much more she should say. 'The way I look at things, I don't think sexuality is ever clear-cut, and it's not something out there that's nothing to do with me. I see sexuality issues on the same basis as any other discrimination: I'm very supportive of gay issues and I've got friends who are lesbians – in fact, one of my friends is a black lesbian.'

'I think I might know who you mean.' I am remembering all the things we already know about Barbara from Liz.

'Well, looking at this assessment, we're obviously going to have to rethink things.' The return to her professional stride is almost effortless. 'We already know from the preparation course that you have a lot of the skills and qualities we're looking for. So the next thing I need to do is to meet your partner. Where is she now?'

'She's at school. She teaches at Broomspring Secondary...' As we talk about Gail, my job, my experiences on the preparation course, I begin to relax. At least Barbara hasn't run away in panic. She seems to want to get to know us, not in a voyeuristic sort of way, but genuinely open and interested, so that's promising...

'I can't pretend to know exactly what to do now,' she explains as she leaves. 'I'm not very experienced and I need to talk to my team. Usually I'd either be assessing a single person or a married couple and you're neither, but I will come back and see both of you together. Is that OK?'

It's very OK with me. I feel I have struck gold. Barbara has a confidence about her and a passion about her work that bowls you over at the first encounter. I sense she is not averse to taking a risk and will be our fiercest advocate if we can win her approval.

She returns soon after with support from her team to begin the assessment, but with more questions than answers about how it will proceed. She is open with us about the confusion in the department.

'I went back and told them, "It's not what I thought... they're a lesbian couple. What do I do about this, then? How do I assess them?" And, to be honest, nobody seems to know any better than me. We don't really know whether to take you to panel as a single adopter plus person living with you, or as a couple. We haven't done this before, you see, you're the first.'

'We know we're the first!' Gail looks rueful. 'One of the reasons that we're doing this is that we know you've had lesbians come through before who haven't been out and that's not doing anyone any favours.'

'I think you're right. From what I can gather, there's

been this succession of women who have gone through panel as "single woman plus very nice woman who is going to help with childcare", or "single woman" whom everyone knew was a lesbian but no one was saying, so it's a bit of a relief for us as a department to have you come forward openly like this. I'm really happy you're doing it this way...' She does look pleased. 'Anyway, what my team meeting suggested was that we take you, Ruby, as a single adopter, because if you were a heterosexual woman living with a man and you weren't married then that's what we'd have to do.'

'Really?' I am genuinely surprised.

'Well, no,' Barbara admits quickly. 'In reality, that wouldn't happen because we'd make them get married. We'd say to them: "You're not going to get through this if you don't"...'

'...But you can't do that with us because we're not allowed to marry.'

'Quite. So you're going to be the main assessee, Ruby...'

'Wow! I've never been one of those before!'

'Yeah, yeah, jargon, I know – and Gail will be assessed as an extra adult who will have significant contact with the child.' Gail and I look at each other uneasily. This doesn't feel very equal or workable, but we don't seem to have much choice other than to go with it. I can't help thinking we're going to end up with the same two-tier system we would have had if one of us had given birth. Barbara can see we're not happy.

'The problem we have is that we can approve you and place children with you, but there's no legal route for you to adopt as a couple. When the adoption goes to court you're going to have to decide which one of you will be the named adopter, and as we're looking at Asian children, it makes sense at this stage to assess Ruby as the adopter.'

This seems so far down the line I'm finding it difficult to focus on right now. We haven't even been approved yet, and who knows if we'll ever get to adopt anyone? I want to hurry her on to the assessment itself.

'We're not too worried about the technicalities of it. As far as we're concerned, we would both be equal parents. That's what we'll tell the children and we're not going to allow a name on an adoption order to affect our relationships with them. So, how do we get started?'

Barbara shows us the blank "Form F's" she intends to complete for each of us, with some sixty-odd questions for us to answer about our childhoods, our histories, our relationship, our ideas about how our life will change with children, our preferences for the ages, race and gender of children we might want to adopt, and the kinds of problems we feel able to overcome. Sitting here with Barbara looking determined to take on the world, this feels real and deadly serious.

'I know it looks daunting. We'll do it in small chunks, don't worry. I'll have to come and see you a few times to get through all the questions. A colleague of mine will be working on it with me and she'll do a kind of second opinion visit at the end to make sure I've covered everything.'

'Is that normal, or is it just because it's us?

'No, no! It's normal. There's always a second social worker.' She says that as if it's obvious, but I realise we are never going to know what she's doing because she has to do it with everybody, and what we have to do because it's the first time they have assessed a lesbian couple and they're feeling their way, as we are.

'It looks fine.' Gail tweaks a corner of the thick wads of printed paper. 'Can we keep these? We'd like to have a go at some of the questions ourselves.'

'Of course you can. You being English teachers, and a writer, Ruby...' She winks at me. 'You'll probably find it plain sailing...'

At the next visit we realise she wasn't serious.

'You've done everything!' She is incredulous at seeing the detail. 'Normally we have to tease these things out of people, like pulling teeth. They just put one-word answers.'

'Oh!' I pretend to look disappointed. 'We didn't know you could just put "yes" or "no". We saw a gap so we filled it in.'

'We've kind of talked a lot about why we're adopting and what we think about things, anyway,' Gail explains. 'And when we did our personal bits, we did them separately, didn't we? And then we showed each other...'

'I don't think I've ever had so much paperwork on an assessment in my life!'

It has been deceptively easy for us to produce convincing answers as two confident, articulate thirty-somethings who enjoy a challenge, like to talk about ourselves and, in our carefree years together so far, have not been seriously tested in our relationship. We are unusually experienced in working with traumatised children, but, like any other couple contemplating starting a family, we can't know how our lives will change with the arrival of other strong evolving personalities in our home. In some ways, we are too plausible for our own good and there are lots of things we don't even know we need to think about yet that aren't on the form, like how to re-tube a hearing aid, what to do when the school wants us to discipline our daughter for leading an anti-war protest we support, and how to cope with homophobic foster carers.

'What I want to do today is talk about what kinds of children you're thinking of, as that's something we need to do when you're both together.' We dive straight in, having rehearsed this one many times.

'We want to have younger children, under-fives really, because we both want to have some time at home with them before they start school; you know, it's about having that quality time with them before their heads get filled with stuff out there, and also because of what they might have been through, we might need that intensive bonding time with them at home.'

'You're thinking of adopting more than one child, then?'

'Oh yes! We thought three because with two they can get a bit polarised, or other people do it to them, like the loud one and the quiet one, or the good one and the naughty one, you know...'

'...And I'm from a big family so I can't imagine just having one child.'

'Well, if you're thinking of three, which is fine, you're going to have to go above five years as your top limit to allow for the age range in a sibling group. My suggestion is nought to seven.'

We are comfortable with this, although the whole process feels a bit odd, defining what we want as if we're making a shopping list.

'And we want girls.'

'Only girls?'

'Yes.'

'Even in a sibling group?'

'Yes.'

'OK. That's no problem. It's quite common for adopters to state a preference for either girls or boys. You do know it's easier to get boys, though? There are more of them needing families.' We nod.

'And we want Asian or Asian dual-heritage children.' Might as well get it all down from the start.

'Do they have to be Asian or part-Asian? I mean, could they be any black children or any children of multiple heritage?'

Gail looks at me and I hesitate. I'm worried Barbara may feel I'm being a bit precious about being Asian and I don't want her to take us being so specific about Asian children the wrong way.

'In terms of my politics about being black, at work and stuff, I want to be as inclusive about it as possible – you know, I identify with anyone who defines themselves as black. But when it comes to bringing up a child, I want to be able to share everything I've got about India...so that's quite different, it's about what I could give to a child.'

'The other thing is, it seems silly when we're such a specific resource for Asian children to use us for something different,' Gail adds. 'Our networks, our local community, Ruby's extended family, a lot of our closest friends, they're all Asian.'

'That makes sense.' Barbara's tone is perfectly even and non-committal as she notes our comments on her sheet. It's hard to tell what she's thinking. 'How do you feel, Gail, about having Asian children rather than white children?'

'I understand that it doesn't make sense for Ruby to adopt a white child, because she wants to be able to pass on everything that she's just said about being Indian. I'm very comfortable with it really. I've spent all my working life teaching black children, mostly Asian, and I can't imagine not being in that kind of diverse environment. I think it would be really odd to be in an all-white family apart from Ruby – and I wouldn't want to do that to her.'

'Do you have any particular worries for yourself about being the only white person in the family?'

'Not really. The only thing I'm thinking is, if the children's link is with Ruby because she's Asian, and she's named on the adoption order, what would happen to the placement if she died? If the children didn't have a legal parent, would they leave Asian children with me?'

'I think it would depend how long you'd been caring for them. If you were their only security after such an awful tragedy, I can't see anyone taking them away from you, but I can see that not being able to adopt as a couple does leave you a bit insecure if the worst-case scenario happens. There's not a lot we can do about that as the law stands right now. However, Ruby could name you as legal guardian in the unlikely event of her death.' She shudders slightly. 'Shall we move on?'

'OK. Well, we're happy to take a child with special needs.'

'Yes, but you don't have to.' Barbara's tone is stern. 'I know there's a bit of a tradition of making single women take children with special needs, but you mustn't feel pushed into that. I don't want my lesbian adopters to be treated as a last resort for the children most difficult to place – you know, "second class families for second class children" – that's so discriminatory on every level. You've got as much right as any straight couple to be considered for any children you want, including babies.'

She picks up our forms and sifts through to the section on special needs. 'Hmm...I see you've put "yes" to virtually everything here. Do you mind if I just go over some of this with you, because I think you're setting yourselves up for a tougher time than you need to? Like taking a child who is HIV positive, for instance. You have to realise that they could get very sick and it could be a lot of responsibility and a lot of heartache.'

I can hear Barbara's good intentions, but there's something about ruling a child out as "too difficult" that feels like writing them off, and I am struggling with this.

'We know that, but it feels wrong for us to rule anything out at this stage when we know nothing about the children who might turn up in the future...We have said we can't take children with mobility problems because of all the steps,' I point out, hoping Barbara will see that we are trying to be realistic.

'We just feel that because of our teaching and refuge work backgrounds, we could be a resource for children who are difficult to place. We've worked with sexual abuse, and neglect, and emotional abuse. There's an integrated resource for children with learning difficulties in my school and we've both worked a lot with special needs...'

'And I went to school with visually impaired children in

the class. In fact, my first boyfriend at school was blind.'

'OK, OK, I get the picture,' Barbara puts her hands up against our barrage of arguments. 'I'll try not to cross anything out. But if you want me to be your social worker, I am going to have to look after your best interests in this. You may think you've got limitless energy, but believe me, any children who have been in care will bring challenges you can't imagine. Why go out of your way to stretch yourselves when it's tough enough as it is?'

'Maybe because we know a lot of adopters are quite picky and some children never get a family.'

'Well, that's true.' She pauses. 'Can we approach this from another angle? Are there certain areas you're not confident about?'

'Well, I suppose I'm not that confident with very young babies as I've never really looked after any,' I confess. 'Whereas you looked after your niece a lot when she was first born, didn't you, Gail?'

'Yes, I had her for two or three days a week when my sister was working, until I went away to university. I think my worries are about children who bottle things up, you know, withdraw. In my family we express our feelings quite openly. I'm used to people shouting when they're unhappy rather than sulking or getting depressed.'

'That's helpful. It's important for the panel to see that you know your vulnerabilities as well as your strengths. A lot of placements break down because adopters aren't realistic about what they can manage.' I feel a bit preached to. We know we have a lot to offer and we want our skills to be utilised. Humility is not our strong point at this ambitious, expansive, boundlessly exciting stage in our lives, and we are too young to recognise the wisdom of her words.

'What about religion? I think you've said you don't practise any particular religion, but you could help a child know about their birth family's religion. Is that right?'

She looks at Gail.

'Yes, I mean I could say that I was brought up a Christian, but I don't do anything with it.'

'So, as you've said, no religion,' Barbara writes this down and turns to me.

'It's all a bit strange this, having to sum up such huge questions in a couple of words.' I hesitate. 'I mean, I suppose "no religion" fits me as well. I was brought up in a very anti-religious environment because of the strong way in which my father rejected Christianity in his youth, but I feel quite warm towards all religion really. I value the role it has in people's lives...'

'You've been listening to that "Thought for the Day" stuff again!' Gail interrupts.

'No!' I leap to defend myself. 'I think it's interesting the different ways people make sense of their lives, and particularly what happens to them when they die. For a lot of black people in this country, their religion is a real refuge and source of hope and positive feeling about themselves, it does lots of good things for them.'

'So you would look at how you could bring up a child in a particular faith...'

'Yes, we'd be prepared to bring a child up in any of the religions of the Indian sub-continent, basically: as a Sikh, a Muslim or a Hindu. And we've got support for that: we would know where to take her, and we've got friends who practise those religions themselves, who could involve our child in their faith, and involve all of us in different aspects like festivals – anything that's going, really!'

'Good. Fantastic. I can't see there being any problems with any of that. I'm really excited! I think we're going to have a very strong application here.'

6

Log jams

Two months down the line, Barbara has abandoned her original tack of assessing me as the main adopter and has started assessing us as a couple, conducting separate interviews with each of us as half of a hopeful parenting partnership and then interviewing us together. She has also interviewed each of us as single adopters, just to make sure she has covered all the angles. If she puts more work into it, asks more questions, makes it more thorough and comprehensive than any assessment she's ever done, she is less likely to run into problems when she presents us to the adoption panel. (This panel has to make the final recommendation to approve or to turn down potential adopters.) But going through it is really like being in therapy, and she is asking us a lot of stuff she would never go into with straight people. I suppose she feels that, with us, she can't assume anything so she always has to ask. In some ways it feels unfair, but we trust her and know she's trying to do her best for us. The grilling we're getting is probably what everyone should get.

Although initially euphoric about our draft forms, Barbara has come across a number of sticking points in the process of revising them and distilling the content into "social-work-speak". She has also been checking things out with her team, who seem to be full of doom and gloom about the prospect of her ever getting us through panel.

'Can I go back to the thing about girls?' she begins ominously, one murky February afternoon. 'I have to ask you this because I think it's going to be an issue for the panel. They tend to think that there's some other agenda going on if you're only interested in girls or only interested in boys...'

'But we've explained all this,' I sigh. 'We feel we've got more to offer girls. Out there girls can be made to feel bad about themselves, particularly girls who have been in care, they're quite likely to have had really negative messages, and we could do lots of work with them and provide a positive environment.'

'And we're a limited resource. You're the one who said we should be realistic about not taking on things we can't manage.'

Barbara raises an eyebrow and lets this go.

'Obviously if you have a birth child you're taking pot luck, but that's one of the reasons we're adopting: we don't want to take pot luck, and we feel we can justify not taking pot luck.'

'I understand all that,' Barbara persists patiently. 'And I'm not asking you to change your main preference. You know I support you and I think you'll be great for the children whom you want to adopt. But if the panel asks me, I need to be able to say you would consider taking a boy in certain situations, otherwise I'm worried you won't get through.'

'Because they'll think we're trying to recruit a little cohort of future lesbians?' I mutter. Gail decides to be constructive.

'What situations?'

'Well...say you had a girl placed with you, and that girl's

birth mother then had another baby, a boy, and you were asked if you would take the younger sibling. Would you consider taking him?'

We look at each other cautiously.

'It's difficult to say.'

'I suppose we might have to consider it, if we had a girl placed and her birth mother had a son...'

'...And your daughter wanted her brother with her...' Barbara embellishes.

'Oh, for goodness' sake! Let's just say yes, we'd consider it. We're not committing ourselves to anything.'

'Fine! That's all I need.' Barbara is triumphant. I have a feeling we've caved in somewhere, but can't remember any more whether it matters. 'Now we've got that sorted, let's deal with the referees. The team have suggested we need a third reference from a heterosexual couple, preferably married, with a child, where they both know about you and you've spent time with their child.' Gail rolls her eyes to the ceiling in disbelief.

'You said everyone has to have two referees. I don't get it. Lucy and Rukhsana are both straight women with children we've spent time with. We deliberately ruled out all the lesbians who would love to be our referees!'

'Yes, but Rukhsana's a single parent, and I didn't interview Lucy's partner. I doubt if he'll want to trail all the way up here from London to see me. I just want to cover all possibilities. So far we've only got female referees, and both Lucy and Rukhsana know Ruby better than you, Gail. It would be good if you could find a straight couple, with a child you've looked after a bit, who know both of you really well. Just to make sure.'

'OK, we'll get onto it.' Behind her confident words I can see the panic in Gail's eyes as she trawls desperately through our networks for this elusive couple. Like the time when Barbara said on the phone, 'Could you find a few more male role models for next week?' and I said, 'Yes, yes,

yes,' and put the phone down and went, 'Oh my god, what do we do now?' We added Gail's head teacher, who lived round the corner and was becoming a good friend, and any male partners of straight friends we could think of. It was silly really because we did have solid male role models in our families, including my father, who would subsequently live with us; lots of women only have women friends, especially feminists, but we felt we couldn't take any chances – this was too important to blow it over a few extra names on a page.

'So, Barbara, when do you think we might go to panel?' I ask, to distract her from further probing about a third referee.

'Ah!' She hesitates as if wondering how much to tell us. We never know with her whether we're getting the full picture, there's so much happening behind the scenes they don't tell you.

'Come on, you've got to tell us now.'

'Actually, we've been talking about the panel because we've got a real job on our hands. There's one woman in there we're really worried about. She's a bit of a fundamentalist.'

'What sort of fundamentalist?'

'Christian. She's black as well, which doesn't help, and she's in a church that's quite extreme about sexuality.'

'Is that allowed? What's she doing in there?' Our alarm bells are bringing the house down.

'Of course it's allowed!' Barbara laughs. 'She's there as a health visitor, not from her church, but she can be very difficult on certain issues and this one is bound to get her going. To be honest with you, I don't want to be at panel having this massive row about you with this one black woman and all these other white professionals just looking on and having a field day, you know what I mean?' I nod, but silently I'm thinking, never mind you being in a tight corner professionally, what about *us*?

'So what can we do? It sounds like, if she's there, there's no way we're going to get through.' Gail voices my dismay.

'Don't worry. I told the team we have to do something about this woman before you go to panel. So we're putting on some equal opportunities training for them around sexuality.' She winks at us. 'That should sort her out.'

'So when's that going to happen?' I don't trust any of this.

'Well, that's the problem. I know I said I might get you into the April panel, but this training is booked for late March, so I think that's a bit tight now. Our hope is that she'll either resign before, or realise on the course that she can't sign up to the department's equal opportunities policy and we can ask her to resign. We're running late anyway because Jane hasn't done her second opinion visit yet – remind me, I must run some dates past you for that before I go – so it's more likely to be May or June.'

'And will it be OK if you sort out the fundamentalist Christian? There isn't anyone else who could come out of the woodwork, is there?'

'I have no idea if it will be OK.' Barbara is always totally open about this. 'The way I've seen panels go, though, I can tell you it will be one of two things: either an absolute nightmare and they'll haggle about everything on your form and it won't go through; or it will go through completely painlessly.'

The problematic panel member resigned after the equal opportunities training and we did identify the elusive third referee, Carla, who had taught with us at Gail's school and remained a friend of Gail's after she left. Her partner, Mike, laid salvaged floorboards in our house and transformed the back yard into a Mediterranean patio, so he had spent a lot of time with us in a monosyllabic sort of way, and their five-year-old daughter had been to the house a few times with him. They weren't married but I don't think that stipulation came up again and we carefully avoided it.

The complication about this reference was that we knew Carla was actually teaching Barbara on a master's course in social work at the university. Carla always raises sexuality very prominently in her work and she told us that Barbara had talked in seminars about this lesbian couple she was assessing and how important it was not to discriminate and how proud she was of what she was doing. We had this whole window on her that she didn't know about and we could see that she was at a stage in her career and her life where she was questioning everything about herself, wanting to improve her practice and feeling really excited about the issues. It made us feel lucky to have got her, but it felt a bit messy when we had to ask her to interview Carla and Mike as our third referees! In the end everybody behaved very properly and it wasn't a problem.

We now wanted to press ahead, but of course the wheels of any official process grind exceeding slowly and we were only one of many tasks in the department's in-tray, and never the most urgent – not even for Barbara. She had a caseload of other people to assess, and adopters to see through real introductions and placements of real children, whereas ours were still only hypothetical. We went on lots of holidays, thinking each one might be our last holiday on our own, and anticipating that we might not go on as many holidays once we had children.

Second-opinion Jane is giving nothing away. She is a thin, tall woman who flows elegantly over the settee in a long skirt and smiles encouragingly at us. We have been dreading this visit for weeks, as her scepticism about our whole enterprise filters through Barbara's tightly reined-in frustration. Barbara will say about some thorny issue, 'I have to discuss this with Jane,' and then she'll come back and say, 'Well, I think this will be alright, but Jane is much more experienced than me and she thinks it may be a problem, so, just to make sure, why don't we...?', and all the time we can hear Jane in the background saying, 'Real world, Barbara! Get off your cloud. You can't say this,' or, 'That will never work.'

'It's really nice to meet you both at last, after I've heard so much about you!'

'We've heard a lot about you too,' I smile back.

'I realise this is quite a brave thing for you to do, being our first lesbian adopters to go to panel. I have lesbian friends myself, so I know what you're up against.' She got that one in quite neatly, I catch myself thinking. No, come on, be generous, she's just trying to put us at our ease.

'There's one part of your form I want to go over, as I'm not sure Barbara's covered it.' I find that hard to believe, as we seem to have covered everything three times over with Barbara. 'It's the section early on about coming to terms with your infertility, I think we need to talk about that a bit more.' We both look at her blankly.

'I'm sorry, I'm not quite sure what you mean,' Gail looks at me for inspiration. 'As far as we know, we're not infertile.'

'It's just that we do advise adopters to let some time elapse to work through their loss issues before they apply to adopt and I'm not sure you've told us about that bit of your journey.' She doesn't seem to have heard. It's like being in a parallel universe and I can't think what to say to bring us back into the same conversation.

'We haven't got any loss issues because we don't know if we're fertile or not, we've never tried to find out,' Gail repeats the same point more elaborately.

'And we're not interested in whether we're fertile or not.' My face is annoyingly flushed with feeling and I wanted to stay calm. 'Adoption is our first choice. We're not like other adopters. We've never, either of us, tried to get pregnant and failed, we're not coming to this as second best, so there's nothing to mourn.'

Jane looks doubtful. I can see she thinks we're in denial and I wish my tone had been calmer. Gail tries another approach.

'Look, if you want to talk about it, let's not talk about loss, let's talk about the positive reasons why we don't want to have birth children. You know from working in adoption how difficult it is for a child not knowing who their parents are, having these fantasies – that's why we don't want to use an unknown donor from a clinic. And there's also the thing of there being so many children in care who need families, especially black children and children of dual heritage. That's why we're doing this.'

'We really haven't ever wanted to have our own babies,' I add quietly. 'We don't mind about it, honestly.' The notion of women who don't want to give birth seems almost beyond Jane's horizons, or maybe it's just that she has no idea how to present this part of our form to the panel because the whole adoption process is framed on a deficit model of failed conception.

'So it's likely that you are both actually fertile. And it's possible either one of you might change your mind about pregnancy in the future and try for your own child?'

'Birth child,' I correct. 'Our adopted children *will* be our own children.' She frowns and I could kick myself. Never try to be cleverer than the professional, they hate it.

'But you can see what I'm saying?' she insists, crisply. 'We usually insist that adopters have given up attempts to conceive, and resolved their issues around this, before embarking on adoption. The last thing we want is the scenario where we place a child for adoption and six months later the mother, or one of the mothers in your case, becomes pregnant.'

'Yes, we can see that.' Gail is being extraordinarily patient. 'We understand you don't want people using adoption like some insurance policy, in case they don't get pregnant. But you can tell the panel we have no intention, ever, of seeking a known or unknown donor and attempting to get pregnant. We hope to be far too busy bringing up our adopted children.'

Jane smiles and relaxes.

'OK. I just wanted to check that out.' I guess she's alright really.

The presentation of our application to panel got put back to June, a full year after my first anonymous phone call to the department. When the day finally arrived, it was almost an anti-climax. Barbara had been right about it going one of two ways, and thankfully it went the way we had been hoping and our case sailed through without a hitch.

'They were really impressed and it went very, very smoothly,' Barbara reported when she phoned us after the meeting. 'I was a bit surprised it wasn't better attended, I think some people must have been on holiday.'

'I thought it would be packed out with our case on the agenda, I'm quite offended!' I joke. 'Didn't they query anything?'

'Not really...Oh yes, the only thing they asked was how come you're Asian with a name like Ruby Clay? And I said, 'The same way I'm a black woman called Barbara Wilson!'

'And they accepted that?'

'I don't think they knew what to say. They've approved you for three children, by the way, aged nought to seven like we said. That means they obviously think you're a strong couple as it's quite unusual to be approved for three straight off like that. Well done! You're the first out lesbian couple to go through our adoption panel. Now go and celebrate!'

When Gail and I have finished jumping around the living room and hugging each other with relief and joy, I remember with some puzzlement the point about my name.

'Why do you think she said that? I mean, it isn't really the same, why she's called Barbara Wilson and I'm called Ruby Clay. Everybody knows about slavery in the Caribbean, but people don't expect an Asian woman to have an English name. They're not necessarily going to understand about Anglo-Indians.'

'Maybe she said it because she just thinks it's none of white people's business asking black people why they've got their names, or what their heritage is…'

'Maybe. But I think she should have explained it properly, otherwise they might think I've got one white parent and one Asian parent. It matters when people are trying to link children with us. I'm Indian. My parents and grandparents and great-grandparents were all Indian, way back to seventeen-whatever when some white sailor called Clay went off to India and had a child with an Indian woman.'

'Yes, but you can see why it kind of is like her. You've got your white ancestor's name, rather than the Indian one, because it was the only way their children could survive. It's all to do with white imperialists having their wicked way with black women one way or another, and what people then had to do to survive.'

'I suppose so. Anyway, it's done now. We're through! Who are we going to tell first?'

7

The ones that got away

The morning after the panel, it began to sink in that we had only jumped one hurdle on the road to creating our family. We still didn't have any children living with us and we had no idea how long we would have to wait for a placement.

'Don't worry about that,' Barbara breezed cheerfully when we asked her, what next? 'I'm keeping an eye out for children for you in the consortium of agencies we're in and I'm also going to refer you to the BAAF register of adopters for black children.'

'How does that work, then?'

'They keep the profiles of all the families nationally that can take black children because social workers usually need to go further afield than the local area to find a good match for black children in terms of ethnicity and religion and language. Also, because a lot of black communities are too small and close-knit to place a child locally: it wouldn't be safe.'

'So what kind of things will it say about us?'

'Just what children you're approved for and a bit about your backgrounds, nothing very specific like your address or anything. Any social worker who picks up your details will have to contact me first. Don't worry, it's very secure.' Barbara accepted we were paranoid about our details getting out, as we knew of other lesbian and gay adopters who had been hounded by the press, mostly in London, and we didn't want a drama like that blowing up in our own town.

'That sounds like a real plus.' I am excited. 'If all the Asian children needing adopters and all the Asian families offering adoptive placements are referred to a central place, then we're guaranteed a match sooner or later, aren't we?'

'Definitely. And I've also got my colleagues in the Black Fostering and Adoption Workers' Network looking out for you. I'm sure something will come up soon. Leave it with me and I'll have children with you by Christmas!'

So we sat back and waited for Barbara's "something" to come up, and went on another holiday or two while we waited. We had an uneasy feeling we should be doing more, but no one ever explained to us what we were meant to be doing. We were never clear whether it would be acceptable for us to do something on our own, or whether there was a rule that we had to do it through Barbara. We were also quite wary initially of outing ourselves to strange social workers or agencies, who wouldn't know us and might be hostile to the idea of lesbians adopting. So we hung onto this hazy idea that all the systems for notifying social workers about children who were available were highly organised, and Barbara must be receiving all this information and would deal with it and tell us as soon as there was anything interesting on the horizon.

The first thing that happened to us did suggest it might all happen really quickly. A social worker, whom we thought was probably a lesbian, contacted Barbara with three sisters she needed to place. She was wildly enthusiastic about us and ready to get on the next train to come and see us. But two of the girls she wanted to place were over seven and we weren't ready at that stage to even consider anybody outside the age range we were hoping for. Barbara had supported us in believing we could have children under five and had led us to believe there were a lot of Asian and Asian dual-heritage babies and toddlers around, so we didn't want to rush into anything. The other thing that struck us about these girls was that they all had the same white mother, and while two of them had Asian fathers, the youngest had a white father. We were concerned that a split might develop in the family if people thought the little one was Gail's and the older ones were mine.

Another thing that happened early on was that Barbara told us about a baby in our own local authority. We weren't very sure about it because it was so close to home and we thought we might even know the young mother. In the end, the baby went to a heterosexual couple. Barbara said, 'It's not a perfect match, but I know the baby will be alright there.' Later, she told us there were problems with it because the mother wanted the child back and we were glad we weren't involved.

Barbara did tell us about BAAF's national adoption newspaper, *Be My Parent*, but she didn't tell us BAAF also had a fortnightly newsletter with advance notices about children who had just become available. For a long time, all we got was the newspaper once every two months. In the end, we found out about the fortnightly bulletin ourselves, and we also discovered *Adoption Today*, the (now) monthly magazine for adopters published by adopters. As time went on, the arrival of these publications came to dominate our lives in an endless waiting game. We would pace ourselves, thinking, 'Oh well, there wasn't anything for us in this paper, but we've got the other one coming in two weeks so there might be something in that.'

Once we started getting the fortnightly newsletter, we did pursue a number of younger children ourselves by ringing the phone numbers given with their details. A lot of the agencies we phoned came back and said they were looking for a Muslim family or a Sikh family, or sometimes they just came back and said they had 'enough enquiries, thank you', and weren't taking any more. We never knew if it was really because I wasn't Muslim or Sikh or if it was because we were lesbians. I found it quite hard to be found wanting as an Asian woman: the implication being that if I were a "real" Asian woman I would have been brought up in a particular religion, speak a particular language and have a proper Asian name. The complexity and obscurity of my Indian heritage was constantly being flung back at me as the weak link in our chain.

I rang a London borough once about two dual-heritage sisters, aged four and six, with the same Asian mother, one of whom had a white father and the other's father was African-Caribbean. I was quite hopeful as no religion or language was specified and I thought we stood a chance of being considered. The social worker was enthusiastic when I first explained my background to her, but went a bit quiet when I explained that my partner was a woman. She took all our details and said she had a number of other families interested in the girls and would get back to us if she wanted more information. She never did. I rang a while later to find out what had happened and they said they were looking at another family for the girls, but thank you for our interest. Thanks, but no thanks, was becoming a pretty universal message.

Interestingly, we were never approached through the BAAF register. At one point, while we were waiting, they changed the system and re-entered all the computer data so that they could match people more effectively, but we still didn't hear anything. We decided it was because of the way Asian children's details were always entered as needing a specific religious background and our details would have been entered as "no religion". Asian children's profiles seemed to be dictated by the religion of their parents, rather than any other needs, and they seemed to be defined in very rigid and specific categories, like "Pakistani Muslim", or "Punjabi Sikh", in a way that didn't happen for white or African-Caribbean children. I knew from my work in the refuge how the so-called "consultations" with communities over definitions of what it is to be Asian were often confined to a small group of men. Teaching in schools, we saw that a lot of what the children thought of as their religion was actually custom and lifestyle labelled as religion by the society around them and their own families.

I don't think any of us, in the department or in our own networks, had anticipated how big an issue religion was going to be in placing Asian children with us. In our assessment, Barbara was satisfied that we could demonstrate through all the work that we had done with children that we knew a lot about different religions, and we could be positive and supportive about the religion of a child's birth family, while not practising any particular religion ourselves.

Another problem we encountered, when we did branch out and start to be a bit more confident, was that every authority worked in a different way, so in one place we'd phone someone who was the central "family finder"; in another it would be the adoption and fostering department; and in yet another place you'd get the child's social worker. The different systems across the country seemed quite random and unfathomable to us as lesbian adopters. We seemed to suddenly hit all the barriers we had ever feared there might be, and a whole lot more we hadn't even thought of.

Christmas came and went and there was no sign of these children we were told we'd have by Christmas. To be trying for something very publicly and conspicuously, and to be manifestly failing to get anywhere, month after month, was hard work for us, and hard work for people around us to have to watch. We started to dread the eager questions about whether we had 'heard anything yet?' and the sympathetic sighs when we hadn't, or, worse, the silent knowing looks over our heads that said, 'What did we tell them?'

'Barbara, have you seen this month's *Adoption Today* magazine?…That family of six Indian girls?'

'Yes, I've seen them, but come on, Ruby, are you serious?'

'Yes, we're very serious. We've been talking about nothing else all weekend. They're all sisters and they're split up in three different white foster homes. That's terrible, isn't it? The magazine says they need a permanent home all together as a family. They're not going to get a better offer than two women, are they? With all our experience of children and working with abuse? I mean, six is too many for a single woman, surely? And I should think, with their history, there are problems about placing them with a straight couple where there's going to be a male carer.'

'OK, OK. I'll give them a ring, but I think you're mad. What happened to only taking under-fives? Isn't the eldest eleven?'

'Yes, but two of them are under five, and there's a seven-year-old, so three out of the six are in our approved age range. Anyway, where are all these under-fives you promised us?'

'Point taken.'

When Barbara comes to see us after contacting the agency, she is very sorry but it looks like a non-starter.

'The woman I spoke to, Margaret her name was, just said to me straight up she didn't approve of lesbians adopting and if your case is taken up by the department she's having nothing to do with it.'

'But is it up to her?'

'No, she passed it on to the manager, and the manager

said your sexuality wasn't a problem. But a manager would have to say that because of what their agency would look like to another agency if they didn't, it doesn't mean they're on board with it. And the other thing about it is, it's long-term fostering, not adoption, which worries me. It means always having social workers, and they can always change things, like what kind of contact there is with the birth mother, that sort of thing, and I just think, is that really what you want?'

'Yes, it is.'

We had moved these girls into our home already in our heads and our hearts. We read the few brief details we had about them again and again, thinking about all the issues they would bring, how they would all fit into our house, or whether we would have to move, what the difficulties might be in their relationships as sisters because of the peculiar way they had been split up into pairs, even down to what kind of car we would have to buy to drive them all around in.

Two months later Barbara came back from a linking meeting at the other agency in a totally different frame of mind.

'I know I was pessimistic about the whole thing,' she admitted. 'These social workers have been such hard work. To be honest, I thought they were just messing us about. So in the meeting I said to them, "Look, just tell me, is my family being seriously considered for these children or not?" and they went, "Yes, but we need more information and we need to meet them". So, I've got a list of questions for you to work on. They're all things you've already thought about, like "How would you explain your sexuality to the children?" and, "How would you provide for the children's religious, cultural and linguistic needs?" And the two social workers who are responsible for the children between them are going to come up to see you as soon as they can.'

'Wow! You sound much more positive about it?'

'Yes, well, I also understand about the long-term fostering thing now. They realise six children is going to be a massive responsibility financially and they can't allocate the kind of resources to an adoption placement that they can put into a fostering arrangement. They don't want to get into a situation where every month you're going back to them for new shoes, or every year you need a new car, so they're allocating a fixed thirty thousand a year until the girls grow up, twenty thousand a year so one of you won't have to work, and ten thousand to look after all the children's needs – I mean, serious money!'

'It would have to be for that number of children, after what they've been through. Are they looking at anyone else?'

'There was an enquiry from a heterosexual couple, apparently, but when they found out the extent of the abuse in the family history, they didn't want to know. And there's this single woman they're looking at, but she's not even been assessed yet, so I don't think she's a strong contender, unless she's got the most fantastic support network you've ever seen. I don't think they were very hopeful about anyone coming forward for the girls, so they tried to look around for someone in the children's life they could link the girls to, and this woman was the interpreter for their birth mother when some of the abuse allegations were heard in court.'

'What?' We are incredulous. 'So it's like – this woman translated for your mum, so what about asking her to look after you for the rest of your life?'

'Yeah! It's got to be better than going to lesbians, hasn't it!'

They scheduled our case for a matching panel in July, so had three months to arrange to visit us after Barbara came back from the linking meeting in April. Waiting for the visit to happen felt like an eternity. It was cancelled twice: once because of some mysterious "legal complication" that was never really explained, and the second time because one of the social workers fell ill the day before. We tried to be patient – we had done all our "homework" and prepared written as well as oral answers for them and we were confident that we had plenty to say.

Barbara kept reassuring us: 'They can't possibly turn you down, even if they think you are the most way-out family in the world: they know that they've got six girls with horrendous histories, and they're really lucky that anybody wants them.'

They ended up visiting at the eleventh hour, less than a fortnight before the panel, and the visit was truly awful. An Asian and an African-Caribbean woman came, and Barbara picked them up from the station and brought them straight to our house. I don't know what they thought of Barbara because she chose to dress in a really "dyke-y" way that day, I don't know if it was a conscious gesture of solidarity, as she had told us before that people often assumed she was a lesbian when she went out with her lesbian friends. Whatever her reasons, you could see the minute they arrived that the African-Caribbean woman wasn't comfortable. She was so tense. When they came through the door, we went to shake their hands and there was this vibe like an Arctic gale that said, no way was that woman going to shake our hands. She wouldn't even make eye contact with us. She just sat on the edge of her seat, really stiffly, and wouldn't have anything to eat or drink, or even go to the toilet, despite having been on a train for over two hours.

The Asian woman was pleasant and polite, but neither of them seemed very clear on their brief. They explained that they were asking us, and the single woman, the same things so that they could make a decision between us. The questions seemed so trivial and obvious that we were a bit thrown. They asked things like, 'Well, there are six of them, so how would you get them all to school in the morning at the same time?' and 'Sometimes they don't like to go to bed: what are you going to do about that?'

They also disclosed some highly confidential information about the girls' difficult experiences, which we didn't think should have happened at that stage because we weren't matched with them yet – we were still just members of the public as far as the girls were concerned. They were probably trying to put us off, but it didn't work. The more we heard about how problematic the girls were and what difficulties the foster carers were having with them, the more committed we became. No therapeutic work had ever been done with them to help them overcome their abusive and traumatic experiences. We got the impression that the foster carers actually found the children's heritage a problem and didn't know what to do with them; there was no sense of any attachment in any of the placements; and we suspected that the foster carers were putting pressure on the agency because they didn't want to keep the girls forever. We asked if the three older girls had been told about us, as children aged over eight are supposed to be consulted about potential placements, but they said not at this stage.

We had expected the focus of the meeting to be on the linguistic and religious needs of the children, but they were hardly touched on. We actually had to force our bits of paper on them and say, 'Would you like to take these away with you? We've answered the questions we understood you wanted to ask and maybe you'd like to take our answers so they can help you at the panel meeting...'

Just before they left, we found out that they weren't even going to the panel. Barbara couldn't believe it, and she made no attempt to hide her disgust.

'You're not going to panel? Who is going to the panel then?'

'Our manager.'

'So why have you come here today? Will you be writing

a report?'

'Well, no, we'll talk to her, obviously, about everything you've said.' The two social workers looked at each other nervously. 'We need to make it clear, us coming here today doesn't necessarily mean that the children will be placed with you. In fact, they may not be placed with you or the other woman.' I could see Barbara was ready to explode.

'The whole thing at the linking meeting was that you couldn't make a decision without meeting Ruby and Gail. And now the people who are going to be making the decision haven't met them anyway! What on earth is going on?'

We always wondered how Barbara got them back to the station without throwing them out of her car.

In retrospect, it feels as if the decision had already been made, but they just felt they had to go through the motions of sending the two workers to see us. Everyone knew the real issue was that we were a lesbian couple, so we couldn't understand why nobody was asking us about being a lesbian couple. Clearly they couldn't bring themselves to say the word, and they knew they didn't need to because they'd already decided that we weren't going to be matched.

Barbara went to the matching panel with an Asian social worker called Usha from fostering, as it was to be a long-term fostering placement. They were greeted at the reception in the social services building by the manager, who said to them, 'Oh, didn't you get our message? We sent a message saying not to bother coming...'

'No, there was no message. Never mind,' Barbara smiled sweetly. 'We're here now so shall we go into the meeting?'

The first part of the discussion was about the single woman and revealed that there were things in her life that meant she would never get through an assessment and should never have been considered.

'Before we move on to discuss the application from Ruby and Gail,' the Chair announced, 'We've got our local authority legal advisor here, who has some advice to give us.' He nodded to a man sitting beside him, who read from a thick brown file.

'We have looked into the legalities of this application because we already know the placement is likely to be challenged in court by the birth family. There's no way that this couple can be considered for these girls because they're a lesbian couple; their application would never stand up in court. Our advice to the panel is this: if you proceed you will endanger the placement, the care order could be revoked, and the children could end up being returned to the birth parents.'

'I don't understand,' Barbara protested. 'On what basis will it not stand up in court? They're an approved couple.'

'Because the girls are of the Hindu religion, which does not allow homosexuality, so placing them with lesbians would be placing them in a lifestyle not appropriate to their cultural needs. The Children Act 1989 states that children should be brought up in a background appropriate to their religious identity and your couple cannot, by virtue of being lesbians, bring them up in a household appropriate to their Hindu cultural background.'

'Excuse me!' This was Usha: 'I'm a Hindu and I can tell you nowhere is it written down in any religious text that there's anything wrong with being lesbian. At least Hinduism is more open about sex than most other religions: diversity in sexual practice is actually celebrated in Hindu temples, haven't you seen the carvings? You've picked the wrong religion here!'

'Being placed with lesbians doesn't mean the girls will be forced into what you call a lesbian lifestyle,' Barbara contributed. 'The girls will be brought up in a perfectly ordinary way like any other children, with help to practise their religion, which will be apparent from the couple's Form F...if we could proceed to looking at the actual application...?'

'I'm afraid there won't be any point in doing that if the placement isn't legally viable,' said the Chair, stony-faced, and no one else spoke; they seemed to be frightened of him.

'But the girls aren't even Hindus,' Usha persisted. 'The birth mother has been through a number of religions with her different partners; she has been a Muslim, a Sikh, and even a Jehovah's Witness at one point, I believe, and the girls have been in white foster placements without any religious input for at least two years now. The connection with Hinduism looks quite weak to me.'

'We have to take the advice of our legal department in this, I'm afraid,' the Chair insisted. Barbara made one last attempt to engage him.

'We've come all this way. Surely we should at least discuss the merits of the couple now we're here?'

'As I said, I don't think the panel needs to spend any more time on this and we have a long agenda to get through. I'm sorry for the inconvenience – we did try to contact you before you set off.' To a woman across the table: 'Margaret, would you mind showing these two ladies the way out?'

'I can't possibly explain what has happened today to my couple,' Barbara said angrily as they stood to leave. 'I insist that you write to them, telling them the reasons for your decision because I can't justify it to them.'

'I'm really sorry,' Margaret said to them in the corridor. 'I know I didn't want your couple, but I don't agree with this. I'm really upset. There hasn't been any discussion about where this leaves the children and what the plans are for them now.'

'Who was that, anyway?' Usha asked. 'He was very autocratic.'

'Oh yes, he's the Deputy Director, very senior,

everybody's scared of him.'

And that was it. Case dismissed.

We complained in writing to the Ombudsman – an institution responsible for redressing very particular procedural wrongs. He couldn't overturn the decision or act in the interests of the children, but he could have found a breach of proper procedure or good practice. He found some minor breaches, but concluded that the agency had been justified in their interpretation of the Children Act. We realised we were powerless against such a concerted closing of ranks by the establishment and could only crawl away quietly to lick our wounds.

The girls were never publicised again. We did hear, years later, from a friend of a friend, who got a job as a social worker in that area and had the older girls allocated to her, that the youngest two were adopted on their own, and that the older ones had a lot of problems in their adolescence. The last we heard of them was that the eldest was in prison.

All that was left to us of the six girls was grief and a fruitless holding in mind, the way we remember children we have once taught in class. Although we never met them, the few individual details we gleaned of them we treasured carefully, as if our having wanted them could reach them still, when they were never even told about us. Stupid, really.

8

Waiting game

When we first enquired about adoption, we looked for a support or campaigning group to join. Being naturally collective about such things, and already embroiled in any number of women's groups, trade unions, black workers' caucuses and lesbian groups, it seemed the obvious thing to do. Before the internet, it was harder to find out such things and I can't remember where we got the information; in *The Pink Paper* maybe, or from friends, but we soon tracked down a support group in London with the very clumsy acronym, LAGFAPN (Lesbian And Gay Foster and Adoptive Parents' Network). We were too far away to attend the meetings in London, but they were planning a national conference in Manchester, which we did go to, right in the middle of our negotiations about the six girls.

The conference was a real turning point for us and I remember it now with enormous gratitude and affection. Until we sat in a room full of other lesbians and gay men all trying to do exactly what we were trying to do, I don't think we realised how alone we had felt, battling away at home against a wall of pregnant pauses and polite refusals on the phone. It had been like trying to join in somebody else's game without knowing the rules. And now suddenly we felt connected and understood, these people played by our rules and their solidarity and empathy were amazing after all our months out in the cold. The conference had been organised by the LAGFAPN London group, working with Positive Parenting in Manchester, a campaign group lobbying for the acceptance of lesbian and gay foster carers and adopters by the city council.

It was an eye-opener to hear people's stories. We shared our own situation with the six girls, which was at a crucial point just then. We met adopters and foster carers who already had children placed with them, and watched their children tumble in from the crèche at lunchtime. We heard from gay men who had been approved for years and never had a placement. We met Kate, a single lesbian from our own city, whose first child, also an eight-year-old girl, was placed with her at the same time as our first daughter, and who subsequently went on, like us, to adopt two more girls. And we met Chris, a gay social work lecturer, who was researching social work policy and practice in lesbian and gay fostering and adoption. He became a good friend and was quietly supportive throughout the most challenging parts of our journey.

After the Manchester conference, Chris, with some other people from Positive Parenting, and Kate, Gail and I, set up a northern arm of LAGFAPN and began organising meetings in Manchester in premises which Chris negotiated for us with the George House Trust, an HIV and AIDS charity. The Northern Support Group, as it became known, has been meeting since September 1994 roughly every two months for about three hours on a Saturday or Sunday with a crèche for the children. Sometimes meetings are held in Sheffield or Leeds, but over the years the most reliable meeting venues have been in Manchester, thanks largely to George House Trust. Hosts of lesbian and gay adopters and foster carers, and prospective carers, have been through the group; some have been in it since the beginning, others only came to one or two meetings.

The group was most important to Gail and me when we were really losing hope after the match with the six girls failed, and in our first few years when the adoptions were still going through. We appreciated equally the support and listening from others, and being able to offer support and listening ourselves. We all learnt a lot from hearing other people's experiences and sometimes we all felt involved in a particular family's journey. Sometimes we weren't comfortable with what we were hearing. Unspoken assumptions of solidarity on lesbian and gay lines were sorely tested along other fault-lines. Gay men could find themselves quite isolated in the group and I'm not sure how good any of us were at acknowledging the general prejudice against men as carers that posed such a huge additional barrier to gay men trying to foster or adopt, even before they came up against homophobia. "Racial" identity was always a bit of a sticking point too. The group was mainly white and, interestingly, those of us who were not white were usually in a relationship with a white partner. Attitudes to heritage and identity differed in the group, particularly to placements of black children with white carers, and generalisations were sometimes made as if stating the obvious, when it was not obvious to me at all that for a black child with severe learning difficulties, her ethnic origin was secondary to her special needs.

We loved going to the group, but sometimes, when we had the children, we found it really difficult. The children often struggled with the crèche, and we struggled with putting them in the crèche, as they have never been children who accommodated willingly or easily to any organised childcare. On the other hand, Lubna made her closest friend outside school through the group and is unfailingly euphoric and starry-eyed about the fact that she and Hannah are both dual-heritage, adopted, have lesbian parents, both have a younger sibling, and both love horses! The emotional power of these connections and parallels cannot be overestimated for either of them.

Being in the group helped us in the long wait for a placement. So did Barbara's irrepressible optimism and faith in us, and the support of the many friends and family members who continued to believe in us. But after we were turned down for the six girls, who quite clearly had no other options, we began to doubt whether anyone outside our own agency would ever place children with us. Around the same time, we were contacted by the London borough that had publicised the two dual-heritage sisters earlier in the year, to ask if we would take the older sister, with African-Caribbean heritage, on her own as they had found an Asian adoptive family for the younger sister. We were appalled that they had split the sisters up when we would have given them a home together, and appalled to think of the impact on the older sister of having been rejected when her younger sister had been accepted, however it was presented to her. We were also indignant on our own behalf. Now that she had fallen into a "hard-to-place" bracket, they were willing to consider what had clearly seemed unacceptable to them when we first contacted them. We told them we didn't feel we were an appropriate placement for a child who so clearly presented as African-Caribbean. We did not say that we didn't trust them or that we were angry with them. The extent of the homophobia we were up against was finally starting to sink in.

We decided we needed to consider other options. Barbara sent a "Round Robin" letter about us to all the local authority adoption agencies in the country, highlighting our unique skills and flagging up our suitability for Asian and Asian dual-heritage children. Arriving outside the usual circulars about new families, it was designed to attract special attention, as if we were a kind of special once-in-a-lifetime offer! She also suggested we apply to train as foster carers, as we would then be more likely to get placements from our own local authority, which had already backed us, at least in theory. Some of these placements might turn into adoption, as foster placements sometimes do. This sounded like adoption by the back door and was a hard decision to make as we were not sure we could cope with the transient relationships inherent in fostering, but we recognised it might be the only way we would ever get to care for children. Our friends Sharon and Sarah applied at the same time and the four of us did a "lesbian-only" preparation course, with another single lesbian, delivered by Usha and a lesbian fostering worker. It worked well as a tailored preparation course, giving us a safe space in which we could be really open about our experiences, thoughts and feelings about fostering, and it gave us a positive focus at a point when we almost felt like giving up.

Gail and I also decided we needed a holiday. We had now been approved for eighteen months and we couldn't bear to spend a second family Christmas at home without the children we felt should have been with us by then. We booked to fly to India in mid-December, with Gail going for three weeks and me for four. It felt like the right, and only, thing to do. Going to India was always quite a special pilgrimage for me and we hoped it would give us a respite from the limbo we had been in for so long.

A week before we left for India, the latest copy of *Adoption Today* arrived and one profile jumped out at us straight away: an eight-year-old girl with straight black hair to her shoulders, a neat fringe and a round face with smiling eastern eyes. From the description she seemed to have South Indian heritage, although it was very confusingly worded and didn't match her appearance. The South Indian city of Madras jumped off the page at me, my father's birthplace and the Indian city I knew best, and the profile said she liked reading, which I identified with, having devoured the entire children's library in my city as a child. She was outside our age range and was in a London borough, not the same one as the two sisters we had pursued previously, but there was a tension at the mere mention of London and we were wary of negotiating at such a distance with unknown social workers. And we were just about to go away. We decided not to do anything till we returned. We couldn't think clearly and were too emotionally drained by eighteen months of disappointments. If it was meant to be, she would still be there when we got back.

Gail returned from India first for the start of the school term and as soon as she arrived home Barbara was on the phone to her about the girl in London. It seemed that she had sent the girl's social worker details of another of her adopters, a single woman approved for older children. She had not thought of us because of the age and because she had another much younger child she wanted us to consider. But the social worker in London had seen the Round Robin being circulated about us and when Barbara spoke to her she was quite indignant.

'Why have you sent me details about a white woman when you've got this fantastic Asian mixed heritage couple? They're the family we want for our child!'

Barbara was lukewarm about us compromising on our age range and couldn't understand why we were not more interested in her four-year-old. The family history of the younger child was complex and unpromising, and there was something about the eight-year-old's interests and specific Indian heritage that seemed to be made for us. Once we knew there was some enthusiasm from the agency and we were not going to have another door slammed in our faces, we were totally focused and smitten. It is hard to describe to someone who has not experienced it, how attached it is possible to become to something as dry and insubstantial as a photo and a few typed details on a form. I imagine it is a similar process to becoming attached to the strange turbulent movements in your body when a baby is growing inside you. But I don't know. I do know the prospect of this particular match once again took over our thoughts and lives months before it got to panel. In March, the family-finding social worker visited us for the first time. She visited again in April with the birth mother's godmother, Jean, whose opinion seemed to carry some weight with the agency. Luckily, she liked us! There were discussions with the child's social worker, her foster carer, her school, her play therapist. There were problems about who could go to the matching panel as Barbara was very sick with the early stages of pregnancy and couldn't travel. Someone else we didn't know had to step in at the last minute. The slow trundle towards a matching panel seemed interminable...

9

'I didn't have feelings then'

Sunday morning, and the bell of our phone jangles loudly through the house. I nearly break my neck leaping down the steep stairs to get it, knowing Gail is an impossible further flight up in the attic, painting.

'Hello?' My heart is beating violently in my chest as I speak. Maya has been staying for the weekend with Jean. Two days ago, she was told that a family has been found for her and Jean has promised to ring us today to let us know how things are going.

'Hello.' The small, high, breathy voice of a child whispers down the line.

'Is that Maya?' I squeak in disbelief. She sounds so young.

'Hmm...mm...' There is a murmur of assent, as if she is nodding down the phone.

'Is it her?' Gail materialises, whispering, at my shoulder. I try to concentrate on the fragile thread of connection I am holding to our future.

'This is Ruby. It's lovely to hear your voice. Have you

been having a good time with Jean?'

'We went to the supermarket, and we had to take Sooty to the vet for her teeth.' There is a whisper in the background from Jean. 'Oh yes! And I watched your video.'

'What did you think?'

'I liked the bit where Gail looks like a marigold!'

'Gail's here too. Would you like to say hello to her?...Is that yes?'

I can hear Jean behind her saying, 'You have to talk, Maya, they can't see you!'

'I know that!' Maya's voice is suddenly loud as she turns to Jean.

'Hello, Maya. It's me, Gail.' Gail's voice is shaking slightly. 'Did Jean tell you we're coming to see you on Tuesday after school?...Yes, at Granny's...It doesn't matter if the taxi's late picking you up, we'll have lots of time...You'll have to think if there's anything you want to ask us...OK...Do you want to say good-bye to Ruby?' I take the phone again. There is a slight listening pause.

'Hello, it's Ruby here again.'

'Is there a moor?'

'A moor?' I am not sure I've heard her properly.

'Like in *A Secret Garden*; that's a book about a girl in Yorkshire and there's a moor outside the house.'

'Oh, I see! Yes, there are lots of moors, miles and miles of them. Not outside the house exactly, but we can drive there in no time.'

'Can I still go to Highfield School?'

'No, but you can go to a lovely school here. It's just round the corner from our house so you won't have to go in a taxi, it's only a few minutes' walk.'

'I don't mind the taxi. I'd like to come and live with you, but I still want to go to Highfield every day in the taxi. It isn't too far.'

I feel terrible that we are taking her away from the teachers who have given her the security and positive input she needed during these difficult years. How can we be thinking of moving her two hundred miles north to live with two complete strangers in a city she has never seen? I am awestruck at her trust and courage in facing this monumental change in her life.

'Let's talk about it when we see you.'

When we put the phone down we are beside ourselves with excitement and the relief of having broken that first ice. She seems to me a very small person surviving bravely in a world that makes little sense, needing a secure home with people who will see the whole of her and stick with her. I hope I don't let her down.

The next few weeks bring an avalanche of milestones, which are engraved on our memories. Our first encounter is in Granny Greaves' cramped front room filled with glass ornaments, plastic flower arrangements and precariously piled furniture. Maya is a diminutive figure in her grey school pinafore and white blouse. Her straight black hair falls over her face and she doesn't look at us as she produces from her satchel a written "manifesto", which she reads out when prompted by her social worker.

'What supermarket do you shop at?' Her tone leaves us in no doubt as to the gravity of the test.

'Well, sometimes Sainsbury's, or Morrison's...' Maya waits patiently as I look at Gail for inspiration.

'And sometimes Waitrose?' Maya nods her approval and continues to read.

'I want to have a goldfish.'

'I'm sure that can be arranged.'

'And I want to have my ears pierced.'

'You have to have social services' permission for that,' Mrs Greaves interrupts, 'I've told you that before, Maya. That's why you couldn't have it done with us.'

'That's all right.' I try to be upbeat about it. 'We'll ask our social services, shall we?' Maya nods shyly and almost smiles at me.

'And I want to be allowed to wash up.'

'With pleasure!'

The second time we met Maya with her social worker, we took her out of school and walked to the park. Reaching a junction with a side road, I felt a small hand slipping into mine as we waited to cross. I wanted to jump up and down and shout, 'She's holding my hand! She's holding my hand!' Instead, I glanced over Maya's head at Gail to check she had noticed and we smiled.

At the park, Maya shut her social worker in the children's playground and for a while wouldn't let her out, as if saying, 'You don't belong with us any more, this is my family'. The social workers had wanted our introductions to be spread over a six-week school holiday as they were worried that, after four years in the same foster placement, Maya would need a lot of time to get used to the idea of moving. We wanted to do the introductions over a couple of weeks in July and move Maya in at the beginning of the holiday so we could spend the summer settling her in before the start of the next school year. We found an unexpected ally in Maya's foster carer, Granny Greaves, a formidable matriarch from the Caribbean, who looked after several of her grandchildren virtually full-time as well as her two foster children. The social workers had been very anxious about Mrs Greaves' reaction, as a devout Catholic, to the prospect of Maya being placed with lesbians. In fact, she was very positive about the match and reminisced to us about the lesbians she had known in her early years as a midwife living in nurses' hostels in Jamaica. We were often proved wrong in our assumptions about people's reactions to us. Granny's was the starkest example, but we were wrong-footed by other people we had been told would have an issue with us, and, conversely, sometimes encountered hostility we had not anticipated.

Forming a neatly timed pincer action around the professionals in the planning meeting following the successful matching panel, Mrs Greaves, Gail and I managed to cut the introductions period down to two-and-a-half weeks, and Maya would probably have moved in less time, given half a chance. Children, very sensibly, like to get on with things and when they know something is going to happen they don't see the sense in hanging around. As we were leaving her to drive home after the first few days of introductions, Maya appeared from her room at the foster home with a box of things she wanted us to take back to her new room in our house.

From the beginning, we talked to Maya about us being lesbians and how it would be for her to have two mothers. We never asked her to call us "Mummy"; we were always "my parents" to other people, and "Gail" and "Ruby" to her, which was not at all unusual in the alternative circles she fell into. In her local Woodcraft group (a socialist equivalent to the Scouts and Guides), many of the children had grown up calling their parents by their first names. Maya was quite clear about what being a lesbian meant: there were big storylines about lesbian characters running in *Eastenders* and *Brookside* at the time she moved in with us. But I'm not sure whether that made it easier for her to explain to other people. She told us that Granny Greaves' eldest grandchild had made some negative comments to her about going to live with lesbians, and I think she may have had a hard time in those last few days in the foster home. Everyone had an opinion about what was best for her, including us, and I don't know how she was supposed to trust any of us.

When we adopted Maya, Gail was working full-time as a teacher and I was working three days a week in an Asian women's training project. I took adoption leave from work and Gail was off for the holidays, so we had six uninterrupted weeks for Maya to adjust to her new home and for us to bond as a family. We took her to visit her new school once before the holiday, when she was on an overnight visit with us, and spent time in the holidays introducing her to girls we knew around her own age who might be important to her. Pushpa, a year younger than Maya, is the daughter of a Sri Lankan friend of mine from the women's refuge group, also a Tamil speaker like Maya's birth mother. Ella, who has African dual heritage, is older than Maya and introduced her to the local Woodcraft group, which turned out to include a cluster of girls who would be in Maya's class at school. Maya would go to Woodcraft, Scottish dancing and other activities with these girls and they would remain her friends throughout her school life, reconnecting with her still every time she comes home now she is an adult.

Because Maya showed great academic promise, we were under some pressure from the social services manager who placed her with us to let her go, if not to a private school, at least to an elite state school. Ignoring the league tables, we sent her to the local primary school round the corner, which had a diverse inner-city intake in terms of ethnicity, religion, class background and family make-up, very like her school in London. Being adopted, being Asian and having lesbian parents were unremarkable factors amongst all the different family arrangements and heritages represented in the classroom. Maya had Indian, Sri Lankan, Chinese, Korean and English friends, who lived with single parents, lesbian parents, grandparents and other extended family members, or between different households for different parts of the week. Definitions of "family" in Maya's peer group are consequently fluid and inclusive.

Getting to know Maya was extraordinarily intense. She came to us thirsty for new experience and there were many things none of us had done before that we wanted to do all at once. Maya baked cakes and painted pictures with Gail. She learnt to ride a bike with me and played all manner of musical instruments, from the recorder and piano at home, to eventually taking up the tenor horn at school and playing in the city's Youth Festival Band. She began swimming lessons at the local Victorian swimming baths and I remember watching her determined splashing up and down the pool from the overheated gallery, delighting in her progress and willing the coach to notice and encourage her. We painted her bedroom together and put up flat-pack furniture, a process characterised by robust self-belief from Maya and Gail and doubtful pessimism from me. We sang along to song tapes in the car and Maya came with a folder of classic songs she had learnt at her London school, which she taught us on long car journeys, and which still echo in my mind when I remember those early days. We were learning as much from her, in every way, as she was learning from us. We planted flowers in pots in our backyard, went camping, had picnics, paddled in streams, climbed crags, and enjoyed simple family time: eating together, making the fire in the evening, bath times, and reading stories at bedtime. I can still remember some of the books Maya and I read. There was one called *Three Indian Princesses*, a retelling of three Indian myths, which we returned to several times; the enchanted forests and wondrous events seemed to echo for me the magic of having Maya in my life. I also remember making up stories for her myself, based on things in the room like clay fish in the bathroom, and a copper ring I sometimes wore that made my finger go green, which we decided had magic powers to rescue an imaginary heroine from alarming adventures. Years later when we were all on holiday in France, we heard her telling Lubna and Saira this same story when she was putting them to bed one night!

The first six weeks before we started a regular routine of school and work were both luxurious and challenging. There was a lot of time to sort out difficulties, and a lot of time in which difficulties could arise, as most parents trying to fill the annual six-week expanse will recognise. We wanted and needed all that space to come together as a family, and in it there were some emotional crises. When Maya was upset about something in those first few days and weeks, she would rush up to her bedroom and fling herself sobbing onto her fine new bunk beds, bought so she could have friends to stay, and so she could finally sleep on the top after years of being relegated to the bottom in her foster home. I remember sitting with her, trying to get her to talk about what had upset her and feeling overwhelmed myself because I didn't seem able to comfort her. Now I think that was more about my distress than hers, and in crying she was actually expressing her feelings in a perfectly ordinary way. At times when she was not overwrought, we talked about how important it was to be able to express feelings and what emotional literacy meant. I was not very good at being emotionally literate myself so Gail was a better example for her than I was. Talking about feelings has remained a theme throughout our journey as an evolving family.

We watch the dinosaur film, *Jurassic Park*, on the television together one evening, all three of us screaming and gasping and covering our eyes at cliff-hanging moments. Maya runs round the back of the settee at the most scary moments.

'It was funny when you hid behind the settee!' I tease her afterwards.

'I remember I watched that at Granny's and I wasn't scared at all,' Maya marvels, in reflective mood.

'How old were you?'

'I think I was about five, but I didn't have feelings then…' Gail and I look at each other.

'You have feelings now?'

'Yes. Lots. And I'm getting bigger, aren't I? Will you measure me again on the airing cupboard door?'

During Maya's four years in foster care she didn't grow much, and it sounds like she didn't have much space for feelings either. I feel angry about the lost four years. It's confusing sometimes, knowing we have the incomparable joy of having our children because things went wrong in their lives before they got to us. If I wish things had gone better for them, I'm in danger of wishing them away from the paths that led them to us. I do wish circumstances had been different for them, and their parents, who were hurt children too once, but I am glad they came to us and I can't imagine them in any other family. We are such a good fit.

Once school started, we were adamant that Maya should see us as equally involved parents. Gail walked to school very early in the morning, and would do all her paperwork when she got there at around seven o'clock so as to be free to come home at a reasonable time in the afternoon. I would get Maya ready for school after Gail had gone out and would also meet her after school two or three days a week. Gail picked her up on the other two days and was often home by five o'clock, even on the days when she didn't collect Maya. Initially, we weren't sure how Maya was managing to explain being picked up by different mothers on different days. We were always open with her and suggested ways in which she could tell her story, but we deliberately left her to choose her own narratives in her relations with her peers. The situation regarding her classmates became clearer after a few weeks when she brought home a letter about parents' evening.

'I don't mind going – unless you want to?' Gail offered, as we scanned the invitation together. We both felt ridiculously out of our depth for teachers who had attended scores of parents' evenings from the other side of the desk. 'She might not want us both turning up. We don't know what she's told them.'

'Maya, what would you like to do about this parents' evening?' Gail asked her when she came downstairs. Maya looked at her blankly. 'I mean, who do you want to go with you?'

'Both of you, of course!' There was not a flicker of hesitation. And that was always how it was. Maya was insistent that we were both visible as her two parents at every parents' evening, class assembly, school play and Scottish dancing performance all the way through her childhood. We both watched her first brave, dazzling speech, aged sixteen, at a "Stop the War" demonstration, and at her graduation this summer, for a few brief hours, it was just the three of us again, celebrating her extraordinary journey and all the work she has done over the years to become the person she is. There we were, sitting beside all the other proud, tearful parents and glowing graduates, whose lives are just like ours, and nothing like ours.

Maya's adoption took eighteen months to get to court because when Rani, her birth mother, returned to her childhood home in India, she left Maya in foster care in London with no proof of her nationality. Until she was legally adopted, Maya was effectively stateless. There was no paperwork to prove her citizenship of any country and we couldn't even get travel documents to take her on a day trip to France, never mind get her a passport. Because of the immigration issues, her adoption case had to go to the High Court, which was quite intimidating for us.

Fortunately, when Barbara asked us about a solicitor, I remembered having been on a training course with a solicitor who had really impressed me, and who had drafted part of the recent Children Act.

'Can I ask Richard Sills?'

'You can ask whoever you want,' Barbara laughed, 'You know more about who's out there than me.'

Richard ended up doing all our adoptions, and the wills to accompany them, and was a great comfort and source of reassurance throughout, particularly with Maya's case, it being the first and the most complicated. He told us that, as I would be the named parent on Maya's adoption order, we could also get a residence order in Gail's name, which would give her joint parental responsibility with me. The court would order that Maya should live with Gail as well as me, and if we ever split up, Maya would not automatically stay with me: any proposed change would have to go back to court, like in a divorce. We felt much happier about this as it seemed to build in more equal responsibility for two mothers. Maya is twenty-four now and we never needed to refer to the residence order, but when it was made it gave Gail a psychological confidence that had a tangible impact on our parenting.

We celebrated Maya's adoption with a party at our house. Maya always flung herself into party preparations with great enthusiasm. She has a wonderful sense of occasion and is very creative, often making her own cards and presents for birthdays and Christmases. We treasure many of the little boxes, picture frames and other gifts she made for us around the house and I still carry the key-ring she made for me twelve years ago everywhere I go. Maya's adoption party was a celebration and a thank-you to all the people who had supported us through our long wait and welcomed Maya into her new life. A lot of lesbians were there, lots of black women friends, some of Maya's friends, and my parents, who in those days were still able to climb the steep uneven steps to our stone-fronted house built into the hillside.

By the time the legal adoption happened, our life with Maya was a year-and-a-half old and she had an extraordinarily full and creative weekly timetable: Monday was her swimming lesson after school; Tuesday was band; on Wednesdays she and I went to the family home of an Indian PhD student to do battle with the 247 letters of the Tamil alphabet and learn basic conversational Tamil for a planned trip to India; Thursday was Woodcraft Folk; and on Fridays she went to a Scottish dancing class with two of her closest friends, and we rotated whose house the three of them stayed at each Friday night. Later on, Maya and

Pushpa went to Indian dance classes on Saturday mornings, first with a local teacher and later with a regional Indian classical dance organisation. Maya opened doors for me into my own Indian heritage that I could never have found on my own. She enriched our lives and took us in directions we couldn't have imagined before we started this journey and we were, and are, incredibly proud of her.

Before we met Maya, we were told we would not be able to go far on holiday with her as she was not used to cars and tended to get very travelsick on long journeys. This caused us some mild anxiety as, after trying to adopt, travelling was our main preoccupation in life. Not to be defeated, we bought Maya wristbands that applied pressure to key points, gave her tablets before each journey and belted her firmly into the front of the car with plenty of music to sing along to. Before long she was as seasoned a traveller as either of us and we were able to drive all over the country and travel abroad, continuing our long-established practice of going away every school holiday except Christmas, including the half terms. Our first holidays together laid the foundations of family traditions that must feel to Lubna and Saira as natural and enduring as the seasons. Maya was the pioneer and helped us carve out an identity as a family that became embedded ever more deeply in her and my connections with India, in the attachment to Spain that Gail grew up with, and the love affair with Scotland that I inherited from my parents. The choices Maya has made in her adult life seem to flow seamlessly from these sources and include a "gap year" in India after her A-levels, and four years at a Scottish university studying Spanish and Economics. Yet the most vivid of all, for me, remains one of our first, modest little forays just beyond the borders of our home county into the neighbouring County of Durham, to the delightfully named Skylark Cottage.

It is February, and so cold at night that Maya needs

extra duvets and two hot water bottles. One day we wake to find snowdrifts where the lane was and no visible divide between the lurid white of the sky and the snow-covered hills beneath. Maya has never experienced snow like this in London and she is entranced. For two days a raging blizzard keeps us indoors by the open fire, doing jigsaws, telling stories, playing games, and cooking *dhal* and pizza, and pancakes on Shrove Tuesday. On the third day the sky is a brilliant blue and there is no wind, you can hear the beat of a crow's wings overhead in the silence and the drip of icicles along the gutter melting in the sunshine. From Skylark Cottage we set off on a long walk to a reservoir, singing rounds along the way to keep our spirits up and shattering ice with our heels in the frozen pools and puddles along the path. A bewildered swan slithers on the frozen reservoir, and hares and grouse scatter before us on the moors. We would have been happy doing this on our own, I think to myself, but sharing it with Maya seems to take it into another dimension, transforming it from the passive repetition of a favourite activity, into something more dynamic, a layering and sculpting of family folklore that we will each take into our collective and separate futures. I remember banks of purple heather and brushing my teeth by a cold rushing river in Scotland at the age of five. Which will be the memories that endure for Maya and shape her life?

10

Squeaky lurki

'Maya, what do you think about us adopting another child?' I am not doing well in the game of Knockout Whist we are all playing and my attention has wandered to other thoughts. The fire is blazing in the grate and a long pink curtain the height of the room is drawn over the front door to keep the howling winter gale out. Maya's reply is cautious.

'I don't want someone near my age.'

'OK, well, someone younger then.'

Pause.

'A baby?'

'If you like…or a toddler.'

'I want a baby I can feed with a bottle.' Gail looks at her, surprised.

'Are you sure about that?'

'Yes. I want a baby sister I can carry around and push in a pram, not someone big…Would I have to look after her?'

'No, that's our job. It wouldn't be like it was at Granny's.' We got the impression that Maya, one of the oldest and most responsible at only eight, had done a lot of looking after the younger grandchildren, including babies. She looks relieved.

'That's OK, then. Ruby, it's your turn. Come on!'

We set the ball rolling to adopt a second child shortly after Maya's adoption finally went to court. We had to be re-assessed as we were now a family of three and Maya's thoughts and feelings were crucial to the process. Megan, the social worker who had stepped into the breach during Barbara's pregnancy, had got to know Maya through the regular reviews before the adoption was finalised, and got on very well with her. Maya was particularly taken with the tiger-stripes shaved into the sides of Megan's unusual hairstyle.

While Megan assessed us, we started looking in the magazines again and almost immediately saw an Asian dual-heritage baby girl called Chloe with a hearing impairment, who was ten months old. Her white birth mother was described as having a history of drug misuse and there was some uncertainty about the baby's development, which we felt fairly confident about taking on. Her Pakistani birth father had been in prison on a long-term sentence since before Chloe was born.

We contacted the agency and they were positive about us and wanted us to take the child as soon as possible. We couldn't move as quickly as they hoped because we were about to go to India in the school summer holiday to make our first contact with Maya's birth mother, Rani. The scenario of hearing about a potential placement when we were poised to leave the country for six weeks was almost a replay of the trip to India three years before, when we had just seen Maya's details and left the outcome to fate while we were out of the country. We feared we might lose the match this time, but the agency agreed to wait for us. Now we had one child already living an ordinary childhood with us, we seemed to present quite a different prospect to outside authorities. Chloe's foster carers were not happy about the six-week delay caused by our India trip as they had a trip planned to the United States not long after our return. Neither of us could change our plans, so in the end we went to India and they took Chloe to the States with them, and all the adoption procedures were organised around our respective holidays.

When we returned from India, it was a mad dash to complete the assessment, go to the adoption panel in our own agency for approval as a family, and then be matched with Chloe at the adoption panel in her agency. There was little of the anxiety and tension we had experienced last time, and we felt valued and respected during the whole process. It felt good to us to be seen as the real flesh and blood human beings we are, knowing the kind of fantasies people can hold about lesbians.

So far, so good.

'We have a bit of a problem with the foster family.' The family placement worker, Gillian, is a smiling rosy-faced woman who exudes warmth and establishes firmness in equal measure. There is something direct and compelling in her eye contact that seems to communicate the unspoken message that she is a lesbian herself. Nothing is ever said. Years later, she and her woman partner join the Northern Support Group as prospective lesbian adopters, and now we all go to group events together with our adopted children.

'They are quite upset about the placement,' the child's social worker, Ann, expands.

'Why? Because we're lesbians?'

'Well, partly. They are practising Catholics and they don't agree on religious grounds. I think it's also that they had hoped, if no one came forward for Chloe, they could put in an application to adopt her themselves.'

'Did someone tell them that?

'Unfortunately, yes. It shouldn't have happened, their expectations shouldn't have been raised, but we can't undo that now. They aren't the right family for her, they're white, and they were told quite clearly that we wanted an Asian family for her that would give her some understanding of her heritage…'

'…But someone also told them no Asian adopters would want a deaf child with that kind of history in her birth family?'

'Yes…The thing is, the foster mother, Lauren, has been looking after her since she was about three weeks old. Apparently she always wanted a girl, and because Chloe was born with heroin withdrawal symptoms and was so ill as a small baby, Lauren has kept her with her night and day ever since she was placed. They're inseparable.'

Great. Thanks, Gillian. The full extent of the opposition starts to unfold.

'And they're a bit upset about the name thing as well.'

Chloe's middle name is Lubna, given to her by her Pakistani birth father. We have decided to swap her first and middle names round so she has an Asian first name like Maya and becomes Lubna Chloe. I have always found it difficult as an Asian woman having an English first name and have sometimes thought of becoming Radha or Rehana, but by the time it became an issue for me it also felt too late. There was also something for me about not denying or hiding the complex history of Anglo-Indians under the British Empire embodied in my European name. But for our children I want the straightforward conjunction of an Asian name with an Asian appearance, which Lubna clearly has.

'So we really are the Wicked Witches of the West come to steal their baby?'

'Funny you should say that, because the eldest boy has actually threatened to kidnap her back if the placement goes ahead.'

No one is laughing as Ann drops this bombshell. I feel the firm ground beneath us sliding away.

Gillian looks uneasy. 'Can we move on to the introductions? We thought they could happen here, if that's OK with you?'

'Why?'

'Lauren and Patrick don't want you to come to their house, and, to be honest, I don't think it would be helpful to you, given how strong their feelings are at the moment.'

'Well, we don't want them to come here.' Gail seems to read my mind. 'With threats like that we don't want them even to know what city we live in, never mind our address. We know all about teenage boys. I've had homophobic harassment from boys at my own school and we don't want to put Maya through that.'

'I'm not sure we can get round this,' Gillian frowns. 'Our practice is to have the foster carers bring the child to the new home and settle her in. It helps the child feel safe and is a way of them giving the child permission to move on. Handover is very important to the future success of the placement, and I'm not sure we would want to compromise on that part of the process.'

'And we can't compromise on our safety when we're faced with blatant homophobia and physical threats to our children's safety.' Gillian and Ann look at each other in despair. 'I don't see why they have to come here. When we had introductions with Maya we did most of it in London, and when we brought her to stay up here for the weekend, we did it on our own, no one came with us.'

'Yes, but Maya was older. She was already going to school every day. Lauren's never even left Chloe at a crèche.'

'So why hasn't anyone been preparing them for this separation? What are you telling us – it can't happen?'

'No!' Gillian's voice is firm. 'It *will* happen and we'll have to find a different way of managing it from normal because these are different circumstances.'

'Thank you.' I sigh with relief at the reappearance of a boundary.

The social workers arranged to hold the introductions in a family assessment centre, which turned out to be a perfect neutral venue and took much of the heat out of the situation. All our meetings happened in a big, light, well-stocked playroom where Maya soon got involved in finding toys to entertain Lubna, and Patrick gradually relaxed and found ways to interact with us around the children. Lauren struggled with the whole experience and has never really got over it. She avoided eye contact with us and her tension and anger were palpable in the room.

I remember I was very nervous about meeting Lubna. Gail was completely relaxed around babies, having looked after her baby niece when she was a teenager. But the idea of caring for a person I couldn't talk to or reason with provoked a lot of anxiety in me. I had depended so much on my facility with language through school and university; through teaching and writing, I was not really aware of the non-verbal communication skills I also employed in abundance. At that stage, I still had difficulty believing in myself as a mother and I had a horrible suspicion that with Lubna I was going to be well and truly found out as no good at it at all, whatever "it" was. I had never changed a nappy or prepared a feed or put a baby down to sleep in my life, not even in the refuge. All these things felt like rocket science to me and I was not sure I could cope with the distress that might result from getting any of them wrong. I had yet to learn that for small children, crying is communication rather than a full-scale natural disaster. I needed to just let myself be an inexperienced new mother of a small child, like any other new mother, but the pressure of expectations from hostile foster carers, watching social workers and my own perfectionism combined to make the prospect of Lubna's introductions a very tall order for me.

The reality was a tiny, slight child with thick, cropped black hair and enormous shining black eyes, who hid in the folds of my *salwar khameez* the first day we met her and then toddled around the room, squealing and pointing at things. She seemed nothing like a Chloe to us, and every inch a Lubna, so we had no reservations about using her new name from the start. She was as happy to be picked up by Gail or me, as by Lauren, and it was soon apparent to us that she lived in a little bubble of her own. This was partially due to her deafness, but might also have been due to the learning difficulties which emerged later and to the unusual intensity of her symbiotic relationship with Lauren. Her deafness had been diagnosed at birth because it was an inherited hearing loss and she had been fitted with hearing aids, which she was supposed to practise wearing for at least an hour a day. But Lauren said she just pulled them out all the time and she and Patrick didn't really believe Lubna was deaf. We didn't argue, but we made an appointment for Lubna to be seen in the Hearing Department of our local children's hospital as soon as she moved in with us.

The first time we took Lubna out of the family centre on her own, she tripped on the path and grazed her face and we had to take her back with a big red scab on her nose. We were mortified, but I think that actually helped Lauren and she began to relax a little as we deferred to her expertise. It was a shock for me to go from looking after an able, independent and quite self-sufficient eleven-year-old to a very needy and demanding fifteen-month-old who couldn't be left alone for a moment and whose every need required advance planning, careful organisation and endless STUFF! As her assertive personality impressed itself on me, I began to lose my anxiety and understand how a relationship is built without words. We called her "Squeaky Lurki", *lurki* being the Urdu word for "girl". Her high-pitched gabbling vocalisations both delighted and concerned us, as we realised that transforming them into intelligible words might be very difficult unless we sorted out her hearing aids soon.

By the end of three weeks of introductions, Lauren and Patrick had mellowed towards us and as we parted on the last day we promised to keep in touch with them and bring Lubna to see them from time to time, a promise that would have been unthinkable three weeks before.

Maya was very patient with Lubna when she moved in. For the first few weeks, Lubna had a disconcerting habit of suddenly grabbing hold of your face when you were carrying her and digging her nails into your cheek. She was particularly likely to do it to Maya and Maya's forbearance was admirable. Once we got her hearing aids sorted out, this behaviour gradually decreased and we assumed it was her attempt at communicating something, but never worked out what. Maya enjoyed playing with Lubna and teaching her things, and through this she also got a chance to experience bits of the childhood she had missed out on. She made the most of all the bath toys, plastic bricks, fluffy animals and musical games that rapidly accumulated in our front room. She also liked to lie on the settee with Lubna, both of them in their pyjamas, drinking warm milk from identical baby's bottles, as requested by Maya, until we discovered that Lubna didn't really have bottles any more. For a short period before Maya outgrew young children's clothes, we were able to buy them matching clothes and I have fond memories (which they may not share!) of the two of them on holiday in matching bright green jumpers and orange jeans, Maya building sandcastles with Lubna on some windswept beach, or taking her off to "explore" forests and streams in hair-raising adventures that became legend.

11

'When is my little sister coming?'

After Lubna's legal adoption, it wasn't long before we started thinking about a baby sister for her and Maya. This was not because we were stubbornly wedded to the original number of children we were approved for, but because, as Maya moved up into secondary school, she became busier with her life outside home, her friends and her many interests. Even when she was at home she was often up in her room doing homework, reading, or ensconced with a friend, and Lubna was left chasing us for someone to play with. Lubna was not as self-sufficient a child as Maya; apart from being younger, she needed constant reassurance and feedback. She was highly sensitive and volatile in her moods. Lauren had carried her around all the time and, even though we encouraged her to be more independent and adventurous, my prevailing memory of her as a toddler is of having her in my arms, and of getting up in the night to soothe her in her cot or bring her into our bed in an effort to get some sleep. It was clear to us she needed a sister much closer in age who would grow up with her.

Then the agency which placed Lubna approached us to say they would like to assess us to be one of their families if we were thinking of going for a third placement. Our own local authority were happy about it as they had a backlog of families waiting for assessment and knew they couldn't get round to us any time soon. So we went on the adoption journey once more, this time as a family of four, and talked to Maya and Lubna about having a baby sister. Maya could see the benefits for Lubna and she was confident and comfortable in her role as big sister. Lubna was immediately very excited and rapidly became impatient. We realised we had a problem. Most young children, when told of the impending arrival of a new sibling, are impatient. But usually you can count down the months and weeks with some degree of accuracy. We couldn't even give Lubna a year, never mind a month or a week, and even though she would have had no real understanding of these timescales, it became increasingly difficult and heartbreaking that we couldn't tell her anything about her little sister or when she was coming.

By the time we were approved for a third placement, Maya was twelve and Lubna was nearly three; she would soon be able to go to nursery for her statutory nursery entitlement of two-and-a-half hours a day. We were hoping to have a third child placed while Lubna was at nursery, so they could have lots of time at home together before Lubna started full-time school in a year-and-a-half. We reckoned that should be possible, given that we had found Lubna only a couple of months after we had started looking for a second child.

Just before our third approval went through, my father was diagnosed with Parkinson's disease. We talked with my parents about what was going to happen when they needed more help and became more vulnerable. After a couple of burglaries, my mother had become increasingly nervous about being alone in the house when my father went out, and she had not been fully mobile or independent since a heart attack five years before. Once we all started talking, we moved pretty swiftly to a decision to sell our current houses and buy one big house with enough space for us all to live together. Eight months later we moved into the house we are in now, the only home Lubna really remembers. Maya was particularly anxious about the move, as, like us, she was very attached to our old home, which we know as "the red house". She made various requests regarding the move: she wanted to have a treehouse, not to move schools, to be still within walking distance of all her friends, and to have another attic room. Amazingly, the new "green" house met all her criteria, although the treehouse is more of a house on stilts built against an apple tree, and her "attic" room is a converted roof space with quirky corners and a dramatically sloping ceiling.

A month after we moved into our new home, two social workers from the agency that had approved us came to see us about a possible match. The African-Caribbean woman, Marcia, knew us well as she had been involved in Lubna's placement, and she also knew Barbara through a networking group for black adoption workers in our region. The Asian man, Naman, was meeting us for the first time and he was glowing in his praise of us as a family. In particular, he was very struck by what a "perfect" (his word!) Asian woman I was in my dress, manners and bearing. I think he was expecting something very different from an Asian lesbian and was surprised to see me in traditional *salwar khameez*, living in an extended family household of a kind he identified with, but had not expected to find.

They wanted us to consider an Asian dual-heritage baby girl who was about nine months old and needed an adoptive family. They were ready to go to matching panel and wanted to place her quickly as she was so young. After their visit, we contacted the foster carer and she gave us a considerable amount of detail about the child's likes and dislikes, what she was eating at present, her sleeping routine, and so on, which we began to rehearse and absorb. We had much more detailed information about her before the matching panel than we had ever had about the six girls who were not placed with us, or Maya or Lubna, but we were not attaching in the same way. We were fully briefed and yet we felt something was being hidden from us about this child. The matching panel was a month later and was preceded by a court hearing the same morning to free the child for adoption. We had been told this was a formality and it would all be over quite quickly, so we weren't surprised when the phone rang at lunchtime.

'Ruby? Naman Roy here.'

'Hello. How's it going?'

'Not well, I'm afraid. We haven't got the freeing order.'

'*What*? Why?' I turned to Gail. 'They haven't got the freeing order.' She exploded silently with the same question.

'I'm ashamed to say that someone in the department seems to have leaked the information to the birth family that a lesbian couple was being put forward for a match at the panel. The birth family's solicitor put up a powerful argument to the judge that this was inappropriate and that the birth grandmother was willing to take the child and needed to be assessed first, and the judge bought it.'

'But she's already been assessed and found unsuitable. You said she's got the older brother and she's not coping with him.'

'I know, I know. And we are sure to find her unsuitable again. Their challenge will get thrown out in the end, but we can't go to the matching panel this afternoon. I'm really sorry. We're still committed to you as the right family for this child.'

'So what happens next?'

'We re-assess the grandmother, and get our own legal team better sorted for the panel, which will probably not be for a few months now to allow time for the assessment.'

'We need to think about where this leaves us. I don't think we can go head-to-head in a court battle with a birth family who are so dead set against us. We've been there before with a foster family and that was bad enough. We've got Maya and Lubna to think of. Anyway, thank you for letting us know.'

I came off the phone and we looked at each other in shock. A small voice piped up from the doorway where she had been standing unnoticed throughout the phone call.

'When is my little sister coming?' Gail looks at me for inspiration and I hold back my tears.

'Lubna, we're really sorry. She's not ready yet.'

'What's she doing?'

'We don't know, they have to find her first.'

'Is she lost?'

We rang back the next day and withdrew from being considered for the baby.

After that, nothing happened for nearly a whole year. Month after month, we couldn't believe there was no one suitable in the magazines, and the agency that had approved us because they had so many Asian dual-heritage babies to place, suddenly didn't seem to have any. Lubna had been with us for three years. It was like being back in the place we were in after we were turned down for the six girls – only far harder because our age range this time was limited to very young children, and far worse because we had to deal with Lubna's forlorn questions about when her baby sister was coming, as well as our own disappointment.

Thirteen-year-old Maya, meanwhile, was getting on with her busy life inside and outside school in a solid friendship group that had moved up from primary to secondary school together. If the rollercoaster of raised hopes and disappointments in our quest for a third child affected Maya, she didn't let on, and there was plenty to keep her busy in our daily lives. At school, she found academic work easy and was talented and creative in every direction she chose to go. At home, her life had become richer and more complicated, both with the addition of Lubna in our own "upstairs" household, and with the addition of my parents downstairs, with whom Maya had close relationships quite independently of Gail and me. They enjoyed listening to her ideas on news and politics, and my father, in particular, spent many happy hours with her expounding on his lifetime passions of philosophy and music.

After the failed match, we did what we always do in times of adversity: we planned a trip to India. We decided I would take Maya on my own, as we needed to do a lot of travelling. We wanted to visit Rani again in the south, and also to travel to the far north-east of the country to find Maya's birth father, who is from a remote tribal state on the border with Burma, now Myanmar, only accessible by special permit as it is in a semi-permanent state of uprising against the government in Delhi. We had made contact with a doctor from this area who lived in England, and one day Maya and I went to his house for dinner. It was amazing to meet someone with the same round Himalayan face and almond-shaped eyes as Maya and I could see what it might be like to be in a place where everyone looked like her. Dr Lotha showed us photos and woven shawls and blankets from the state, where every tribe has its own design, a bit like tartans in Scotland.

'Shall we ring your grandfather?' he asked her, as we sat flicking through photo albums in their immaculate front room. Maya looked at me, alarmed. I couldn't believe our luck. I had been racking my brains as to how we would get a special permit to enter the state without someone to vouch for us in the area. A family contact would make all the difference. 'He used to be a minister in the state government and he runs his own school. Everybody knows him. It's easy to get his number.'

'That would be really helpful if we could. Don't worry, Maya, I'll do the talking.'

'I can't promise it will go well.' Dr Lotha lowers his voice as we go out into the hallway so Maya can't hear. 'His sons have brought much disgrace to him with their drug problems and he has been quite ill with his heart from the stress. He may not wish to be reminded of their mischief by a child born outside marriage.'

'I understand, but it's worth a try. I think he will want to see her because he once offered to adopt her himself.'

When the London social workers first decided to find a family for Maya, they contacted her paternal grandfather and he said he would adopt her. He had an adopted daughter already and, as a wealthy patriarch who owned a boarding school in the main town, he also had several children from his tribal village already in his care in a kind of informal adoption arrangement, which is very common there. But when the London borough arranged for a female social worker from Delhi to carry out an assessment, he was deeply affronted and sent her packing: firstly, because he resented being vetted when he had made such a grand, charitable gesture; secondly, because he refused to be interrogated by a woman; and thirdly, because Indian officials of any sort were loathed in the region. The London agency abandoned that line of enquiry.

It took the doctor a while to get an international connection, but suddenly he was talking in his own language, with the odd Hindi or English phrase surfacing briefly in the torrent of staccato vowels and consonant clusters. He stopped abruptly and handed the phone to me.

'He is very happy you are coming to his country. Here you are. Speak, speak!'

'Hello, Mister Niu, I'm Ruby, Maya's adoptive mother.'

I speak loudly and slowly through the disorientating echo on the line.

'Hello, hello, Ruby, I am honoured that you do this great thing for my family. I had wanted very much to help Maya but I couldn't get any information about her. When you land in Delhi, you telephone me and I will explain everything about where to get the permit for coming here.'

'Actually, we're flying to Madras to see Rani. But there's a Foreigner's Registration Office there so they may be able to do it.'

'I don't think so. Then if you are not going to Delhi, you will have to do it at the last, in Calcutta, before you get the plane. Don't worry, it can be done.'

I am not worried and I know it can be done. In fact, I managed to persuade a very kind immigration official in Madras to issue us with a permit on the grounds that Maya's grandfather had a serious heart condition and this might be the only chance she would ever have to meet him.

I always find it difficult getting on a plane and leaving any part of my family behind. Being separated by oceans and continents produces a state of anxiety in me that no amount of breathtaking scenery and fascinating encounters can soothe. Leaving Lubna was particularly hard on that occasion, as I had not spent more than a few hours away from her in the three years she had been with us. Even before we had left England I was pining. As Maya and I waited to board our flight to Mumbai in the departure lounge, I caught sight of a dark, curly-haired toddler running in and out of the sprawled luggage belonging to a big Indian family, and I felt a physical ache for Lubna's tiny body in my arms, the trusting weight of her head sinking heavily into my neck as she falls asleep on my shoulders.

The next four weeks were amazing and unforgettable, particularly our week on Maya's grandfather's farm, complete with cows, pigs, geese, pet monkey and a lake full of fish. The farm was surrounded by quiet, sunlit groves of teak trees and betel nut palms and we were told that wild elephants roamed in the jungle beyond. Maya's grandfather prided himself on having entertained foreign dignitaries in the past, at the height of his political career. We were very well looked after, but our status as privileged guests sometimes came at a price. Maya's most challenging moment, as a strict vegetarian, was hearing the chicken being slaughtered for a special celebratory meal to welcome her into the tribe. She couldn't bear to eat the meat, so I had to make extra efforts to show our appreciation of so much hospitality.

'You must try our greatest local delicacy – mulberry,' Mr Niu urges me at the end of our welcome meal. After some commotion in the kitchen, which is across the yard, I am presented with a cluster of small, curled, greyish forms, which could plausibly be a type of berry, but I am confused by their extremely powerful acrid taste.

'What exactly is this?'

'Mulberry,' he repeats, amazed at my slowness. 'You know, the mulberry tree? We make silk from these ones.'

'Silkworms!' I look at Maya in horror as she laughs into her napkin. 'I'm eating roasted silkworms!'

The next day, we visit Maya's tribal village in the high mountains, a six-hour drive up a treacherous winding road between dense forest and precipitous cliffs. Just as we are about to set off, a man in a khaki uniform with a large rifle slips onto the bench seat in the front of the car beside Maya's grandfather and his driver.

'Excuse me, who is he?' I have no desire to travel with a gun of any sort.

'This is my guard. Yesterday on this road, a bus was blown up by the rebels. Very tragic. The bus was full of school students travelling back to their villages for Christmas, four of them were killed. Because I am a politician, the police give us an armed guard for our protection.'

'Won't that make us more of a target?'

'No, no, not at all. You don't worry. It's very safe. There are many police in the area now. The rebels won't come back for a long time.' I am not reassured, but we are already speeding out of town trailing clouds of red dust, and our visit to the highlands is indeed without incident, apart from more slaughtered chickens and a lot of conspicuous military activity.

Maya's birth father, Longso, a tall, brooding man, takes us out for a drive to see the ancient tribal longhouse and the forested hills beyond the town. He is a little awkward with Maya, firing questions at her about how she is doing at school, between long silences. He gives Maya a tribal blanket and buys us drinks and noodles in the best Chinese restaurant in town, but Maya prefers to spend time with her grandfather's new young wife and the wife's four sisters, sitting on wooden benches around the stove of their village home.

At the end of our odyssey, I am relieved to spot Gail's face amongst the crowds of Pakistani families waiting for a big flight from Islamabad in the Arrivals Hall at Manchester Airport. Lubna in the buggy is lost to view, but is soon back in my arms. On the way home, Maya is non-committal about having met her birth father, but she is excited about all the tribal spears and blankets she has brought home, and her pride in her unusual heritage shines through. She has been surrounded by people who look like her and has been celebrated as a lost child returned to the fold in her own tribal village, still locked in an ancient way of life high on green terraced hillsides beneath the snow-capped peaks of the Himalayas.

When we get back to the house, Gail draws me into the kitchen out of earshot from Maya and Lubna.

'You'll never guess what happened while you were away! They've rung us about a child!'

'Wow! Tell me all about it!'

'Well, when they first rang I just said forget it...'

'*What?*'

'She is a five-month-old baby, given up voluntarily in the hospital by the birth mother, and she is only accommodated...'

'Oh, that's hopeless.'

'Exactly. There is no care order or anything, the birth mother just left her and asked them to find adopters for her. So I said, that's a non-starter for us, if the birth mother has the right to choose the adopters herself, who's going to choose lesbians? They said not to be so pessimistic, we should give it a go, but I told them not to bother. In the end, they went ahead anyway and showed our details to the birth mother, together with the details of some other couples.'

'I suppose it can't hurt.'

Gail is impatient to get to the crunch line and brushes aside my interruptions.

'No. Anyway. The best bit is – she's chosen us!'

'NO!'

'Yes, yes, yes!' She jumps up and down with glee and I cannot believe it, there has to be a snag.

When the children are finally in bed, Gail shows me everything Marcia has given her about the baby. Her white birth mother is in a hidden relationship with a Pakistani taxi driver, who has an arranged marriage. She is quite young and has already had three children with him. She apparently didn't know she was pregnant with a fourth child, and when she went into labour and gave birth unexpectedly, she told the hospital she couldn't take another child back into the insecure situation she was in. She made her own "person spec" for the adopters she wanted, including: must have other children; must be educated and have lots of books; and must be able to tell the child about Islam without bringing her up as a practising Muslim. We ticked more boxes than any of the heterosexual couples she was offered, so we got the job of having her daughter in our family! Her profile is a perfect match for Lubna, even down to being born in the same county. The gap of four years between them is bigger than we had hoped for, but is more than made up for by the delightful prospect of having the babe-in-arms Maya originally asked for.

'It always happens when we go to India!'

12

Buddha on a blanket

'She's in here,' Pat, the foster carer, wipes her eyes with a tissue as she shows Gail, Maya and me through her kitchen and into her living room. 'I'm sorry. I didn't want to cry, I just get so emotional about all this. I wish they'd taken her months ago.'

When we first met Pat, we thought for a few minutes we had another Lauren and Patrick situation on our hands. She sat in the planning meeting after the successful matching panel with her head down, shocks of blond hair covering her eyes, sniffing loudly into a succession of tissues that she screwed up and stuffed into her open handbag. When she was finally able to speak, her voice was hoarse and thick with emotion.

'It's nothing personal about you two, it really isn't. I just never should have been given a baby. When I did the training I said I didn't want anyone under two as I get too attached – and what did they go and give me as my first placement? A newborn baby straight out of hospital – I mean, I ask you! They've not got the sense they were born with, some of these social workers, present company excepted, of course! They promised me they would move

Baby Lulu – I know that's not what you're going to call her, but we couldn't call her by her real name with us having a daughter with the same name. Anyway, they said they could move her really quickly, what with the birth mother not objecting, but then the first social worker changed jobs and they didn't allocate anyone else for months till Bernie started. You could have had her when she was about three months old if they'd got a move on...'

'Well, we're here now,' Bernie saw her chance to interrupt the flow, 'So let's talk about the introductions.'

Everyone agreed there was no point in prolonging introductions for such a young child. The plan was to meet her and move her into our home within the space of five days, during which time we had the minor complication of Maya going on a school trip to France. We decided not to tell them about the even bigger potential hurdle, that we intended to take our new baby to a house with no electricity on a remote Scottish island four days after she moved in with us. We didn't want them to postpone the introductions for another month, and we knew our regular Easter holiday on the island would be a perfect opportunity for us all to bond – we were just not sure anyone else would understand. After a fortnight's isolation by the sea, Saira might be confused about where she now lived, but she would be in no doubt about who was in her new family.

'Now then, Baby Lulu, look who's here! It's your big sister, Maya, and your new mums!' Pat's husband, Dave, leans his gruff, laughing face down from the settee towards a small round form planted solidly in the middle of a blanket on the floor. She has been dressed in a pale pink playsuit with a teddy bear embroidered on the padded chest and she looks up at us seriously with clear brown eyes.

'Hello, Saira!' I crouch down to meet her gaze at floor level. She doesn't smile, and she doesn't cry. She just looks, fearlessly, with quiet interest, waiting to see what will come next. Her Pakistani heritage must be located, like Maya's, in the foothills of the Himalayas, as she has the rosy cheeks and almond-shaped eyes of a Tibetan baby. She sits motionless on her blanket, grounded as a Buddha, her chubby legs curled in front of her, blowing me away with the ancient wisdom in her gaze.

In the days that followed, we discovered a placid, easygoing child, suddenly fragile when we least expected it, but mostly sunny and calm. I remember feeling devastated in one of those fragile moments the first night Saira moved in. I was giving her a bath and something I couldn't identify frightened her in our bathroom. Her eyes widened, her bottom lip started to quiver and her little round face crumpled in despair. I felt so unbearably guilty at not being Pat and could not believe we had torn her away from the only safety she had ever known. I tried to distract her with a bright bath toy, but had to hand over to Gail who came to see what was wrong and, clocking my distress, soon had the situation in hand and Saira playing happily with soap bubbles again. When Saira was very young, and mostly before she could talk, she would have occasional moments of terror in the night when she would wake up screaming and be quite inconsolable. At these times, it seemed as if she didn't know who I was and the loneliness of her terror was heartbreaking. Now when she has nightmares she calls out, 'Mum!' to me, and she knows it's me she's calling.

Extracts from my holiday diary, Easter 2001:

> *Saturday: Got up 2.00am, packed car and made up 10 bottles for S. Set off 3.00am. Breakfast in Glasgow. Ferry to the island at 1.00pm. Problem with Calor gas cooker when arrived at house – S drank all 10 bottles of milk – help! Rescued by man at next farm. Told me his life story while fixing new gas bottle.*

Monday: Got up early – sunny day. Took L out walking along cliff to find beach with "soft sand". Mobbed by hungry sheep, who thought we were bringing hay. Found beach and L took all her clothes off and ran into ice-cold Atlantic! Back to house for lunch and we all sat in sun in the garden. S happy to sit on blanket and watch L and M playing football.

Wednesday: Got up early with S. Played on floor in library till everyone else woke up. Later, all went to the beach. I took S in sling. Sat on beach in sunshine, S on blanket, L made sandcastles, M swam in sea – freezing! Seals came over from rocks to watch her. S fell asleep in sling on way home.

Thursday: G and M made pineapple upside-down cake and baked bread in Rayburn. L invented her own baby, "Shankenana", who promptly died! (Is she trying to tell us something?!) G and L went for a long walk and saw three newborn lambs. L fell asleep after walk, but was up in the night – not good.

Sunday: Easter egg hunt in garden. L, M and I went to swimming pool. M read book and watched L and me in Under-Sevens Fun Session. Phoned Mum and Dad on way back, which made L homesick – oh dear! Took her for walk across fields and down to other beach and saw seven swans – felt better. Got up in the night and saw full moon shining on sea.

Wednesday: G and M did big walk along cliffs to lighthouse. L, S and I played in garden. Made a fire in house when wind got too cold for S. Waited for wanderers to return. Hilltop path too tame for M: made own way along coast and met G at the bothy.

Friday: Walked to bothy on my own. No one on the path all day. Deer on the hills. Later, packed and tidied up.

Saturday: Started raining as we left the house and rained all day. M said island was crying because we were leaving! Ferry at 3.30pm. Arrived home 11.30pm. Dad had put hot water bottles in the children's beds!

That was the beginning of the rest of our lives as a family. Apart from Saira's adoption going to court a few months later, that was the end of all the assessments and panels, case reviews and social worker visits. It didn't mean pretending our children weren't adopted, but it did mean we didn't have to depend on anyone else now to arrange our family for us.

13

Tapestries

Each of our children came to us with a "life story book", telling them about their birth family and the circumstances of their birth and containing a brief narrative of their life up to that point. Each book includes whatever pictures could be found or taken by their social worker to bring their past to life, including pictures of their birth parents and any siblings. Maya also had a considerable body of information and documents from Rani's family passed on to her, which she looks after herself. Lubna and Saira have a large photo album each, which we keep in a cupboard in the living room and which they get out occasionally to show to friends or visitors, or just to look through themselves. They are quite interested in this early information, but if they feel in reminiscent mood are much more likely to demand a viewing of old videotapes of holidays and Christmases when they were small. They watch these badly filmed clips with total absorption and endless delight, fascinated by their younger selves. Both sources are important in helping them integrate everything they know about themselves into a picture that makes sense. We have tried to weave into their lives with us as many of the strands of their early histories as we had access to, and knew about, in the hope that they will take into adulthood a rich tapestry of knowledge, memories and connections to support their sense of themselves.

We spent a lot of time working out the finer points of our children's names on their adoption certificates, as we recognised the importance of names in expressing a person's history and identity. Choosing the children's names had tremendous potential to either contribute to a coherent narrative for them, or confuse and fragment them. Maya kept all her original names, because she had been using them for so long when she came to us that they were an essential part of her. We did add my surname after Maya's on her adoption certificate, because we wanted to tie her clearly to me on her passport the first time we took her to India to have contact with Rani. She never used my surname anywhere else, and when our anxieties about travelling abroad with different names in our passports had subsided, we removed my surname from her adoption certificate by deed poll.

We swapped Lubna's first and second names around so that Chloe became her second name. We also kept Lubna's birth father's Asian surname as a middle name, so she would have a full Asian name if she chose to use it when she grew up. When it came to her adoption, it was Gail's turn to be the named adopter, and we gave her Gail's surname as a link to Gail that people would accept easily, given that her Asian appearance already offered a visible link to me. So Lubna ended up with a grand total of four names: Lubna Chloe Anwar Moore!

When Saira was placed with us she had an English first name, which had never been used as the foster family called her "Baby Lulu". We couldn't call her "Baby Lulu" for much longer as, apart from anything else, she was soon not going to be a baby, so before she came we sat down as a family to think of an Asian first name that would have a different initial from the rest of us and would fit in well with Maya and Lubna. We came up with Saira, and kept her English first name as her middle name. As with Lubna, we included her birth father's Asian surname as another middle name and gave her Gail's surname, so that she and Lubna would be clearly identified as sisters as they moved through the same schools. So she, too, has four names: Saira Rosie Khan Moore.

Each time we went to court, one of us was named as the legal adopter on the child's adoption certificate, which replaces their birth certificate. At the same adoption hearing, we also applied for a residence order in the other partner's name to give us both parental responsibility in law. We took it in turns: I was Maya's named adopter, Gail was Lubna's, and it was my turn again with Saira. The residence orders for the other partner did what we needed in giving us both authority to take the children out of the country on our own and sign all sorts of documents like school transfer forms, medical authorisations for operations, and so on. But residence orders only applied up to the age of sixteen. Once Gail's residence order for Maya lapsed, Maya had no legal connection to Gail or Gail's family. The same would have been the case for Saira, and for Lubna with me, if the law had continued as it was. The permanent legal linking of each child to only one of us also meant that only Maya and Saira were siblings in law, through having me as their adoptive parent, and neither was linked to Lubna as a sibling because she had a different adoptive parent. It also meant they all had different legal relationships to the respective sets of grandparents and extended families.

None of this mattered to us on a daily basis. We carried on our lives as a family as if we were all completely tied to each other like any other family, and the younger children were not even aware that only one of us was named on their adoption certificates. After each new adoption, we remade our wills to cover all the gaps and name everybody who needed to be connected to our children in the event of our deaths.

The Adoption and Children Act 2002, which came into force in 2005, allows joint adoption by unmarried couples so that both partners can be named as adoptive parents on the child's adoption certificate. It is not a legal measure designed specifically for lesbian and gay couples as it applies to any unmarried partners, and it often gets confused with the Civil Partnership Act 2004, which also came into force in 2005. People sometimes think, mistakenly, that lesbian and gay couples can now only adopt together in law if they have a civil partnership. They also think, mistakenly, that before this legislation lesbian and gay adoption was illegal, which was clearly not the case as many of us were doing it! It was only that lesbian and gay couples, like other unmarried couples, couldn't both be named as adopters on an adoption order.

When the law changed, Gail and I couldn't wait to go back to court to put in some of the missing connections and formally ratifiy the informal relationships we were living every day. Sadly, Maya was already too old to be included and will always have only me as her legal parent. But going back to court to re-adopt Lubna and Saira as a couple has enabled us to connect them legally as full siblings, and that ties Maya in as their sister through her link with me. These legal connections are more than just "bits of paper": they are the cement securing the foundations of our lives as a single unit, a family, a whole that is more, and other, than the sum of its parts.

Despite all our efforts to parent equally, I do wonder sometimes if those earlier subtle differences did not have some unconscious effects somewhere on Gail and me in the complex attachments we have forged individually with our three children.

We never had to sit down with any of the children and

have a Big Talk about adoption or about us being lesbians, because there was never anything secret or undisclosed that needed to be revealed. Because of her age and ability, Maya understood what it meant to be adopted by lesbians when she came to us. With Lubna and Saira, we made sure we talked about them all being adopted, and about us being lesbians, regularly and openly from the beginning, so they were hearing the words as they were learning to speak and absorbed the concepts like children do, through the natural contexts in which they arose. For them, it was as normal to be adopted, and to have two mums, as it was to have brown skin or to live with your grandparents. Maya helped a lot in that too, and probably teaching her sisters about their family also helped her to consolidate her own identity as the adopted daughter of a lesbian couple. One of the few complaints she had was about the intensity of having two mums, which was particularly acute for Maya when she was the only child with two very active and involved parents.

Knowing other lesbians who had adopted was helpful to the children and was particularly significant for Lubna, whose best friend, Hannah, and Hannah's brother, Damien, were adopted by a lesbian couple we knew initially through the Northern Support Group. Bev is dual-heritage African-Caribbean and Helen is white; they adopted Hannah and Damien when the children were six and four. Lubna is only three months older than Hannah and they made friends instantly and permanently. They have both developed a passion for horses, but the strength of their friendship lies in the affirmation they each receive from seeing their own life reflected in the other's.

'It's so amazing that Hannah and I have everything the same!' Lubna tells me, beaming at this sudden revelation as we drive home from the stables. 'She's adopted, like me. She has lesbian mums, like me. She's dual-heritage, like me. She likes horses and wants to work with animals, like me. She has a younger brother, and I've got a younger sister. And she needs help at school, like me! Maybe we're twins!'

The occasions on which our being lesbians have caused the children or us significant difficulties are few and far between, as we have generally been surrounded by supportive people and institutions. The staff at the Hearing and Speech department of the local children's hospital have known Lubna since she was sixteen months old and accepted us as her parents from the beginning, but on one occasion when we took her to hospital she had to see a different consultant.

We have barely sat down in the room when the woman consultant demands quite abruptly: 'Which one of you is the mother?'

'We both are.' Gail is calm, and wary.

'Yes, but which one of you gave birth? I need to know who is actually the mother.' Her impatience suggests she has dealt with lesbian couples before and is not impressed with this state of affairs.

'We both are,' Gail persists. 'She's adopted. By both of us.'

'So neither of you gave birth?'

'That's right.'

She dismisses us with a sniff and proceeds with her investigation.

Maya came to us with a strong sense of being black, which she had acquired in her foster family and in the multi-ethnic environment of her London primary school, where racism was both visible, and challenged. She has always talked freely about her experiences of racism and about her own identity as a young Asian woman. We talked a lot about skin colour and heritage when Lubna and Saira were small, even before they could talk, so that seeing themselves, Maya, and me as "brown" and Gail as "pink" was as natural as learning the names of all the other colours. As they grew up, we used more complex and abstract language to explain their heritage. Lubna identifies particularly with the term "dual-heritage" at the moment, whereas Saira sees herself and her friend, Leah, who is dual-heritage, as "brown", and her African-Caribbean friend, Natalie, as "black". Both Lubna and Saira understand that their birth fathers are Pakistani, and were brought up as Muslims. They also know that my parents were born in India, and they met Maya's birth mother on their first visit to India, when Lubna was six and Saira was only two and just out of nappies. They adapted to life there with the easy acceptance of children who are used to travel. Two years later, we returned to catch up with Maya and her friend, Devi, on their gap year, learning classical Indian dance, and teaching in a slum school, in Mumbai. When Lubna was ten and Saira was six, I took them to Pakistan on my own, so they would have a collection of memories and images to attach to the word "Pakistani" when describing themselves.

Lubna and Saira both gravitated towards other black children from their first days at nursery when they were three. Lubna was inseparable from an African-Caribbean girl called Sophie for the entire duration of her time in nursery and they did everything together, to the extent that Sophie even wanted to have hearing aids like Lubna. Saira was similarly inseparable at nursery from a girl with dual African-Caribbean and white heritage, called Leah. The clarity and single-mindedness with which these little girls found each other out, aware that they shared something and felt safe together in majority white groups, confirmed my own vivid early memories of spotting the one or two other black and Asian children in a whole school of white children.

Lubna will often spot racism, or will ask us if we think someone is being racist. She struggles creatively to reconcile the conflicting messages she receives in her complex position as a child with Muslim heritage who doesn't practise a religion, as a deaf child in a hearing family, as a daughter of lesbian parents in a teenage world of enforced heterosexuality, and as a Pakistani child with siblings and parents of mixed Pakistani, Indian and white heritage.

'Please don't wear Asian clothes when you come to school tomorrow,' she asks me one day.

'Why?' I am shocked. 'Are you ashamed of being Asian or something?'

'No…It's just that people might think I'm a Muslim and then no one will ask me out.' I look puzzled and she elaborates further. 'People think Muslim girls aren't allowed to go out with boys, so if they think I'm a Muslim they won't ask me out, even if they like me, and then I'll never have a boyfriend.'

'You're too young to have a boyfriend.' My reflex response is both untrue and unhelpful, but I am struggling to know what to do with her request. I have prepared myself for her to be embarrassed at some stage by me being a lesbian; I had not anticipated this. 'Millions of women in India wear *salwar khameez* and they're not Muslims.'

'Everyone I know who wears Asian clothes is a Muslim. I can tell on Facebook from what someone's wearing, and I'm always right, when I click on their profile it says Muslim.'

'Which just shows you can't trust Facebook! Lubna, you can't tell a person's beliefs from their clothes. That's stereotyping.'

'I know, but it's what people think! You don't understand…' I can see that challenging these assumptions with Lubna will have little effect on her peer group. The next day I wear an Indian *khameez* over Western trousers. She is satisfied and I don't feel completely swept under the carpet.

We knew we had to weave into the story of Lubna's life

positive strands about her deafness and her learning difficulties. Thanks to the local children's hospital, Lubna wears her state-of-the-art digital hearing aids all the time and has learnt to speak very clearly. We fought for her to have a statement of special educational needs put in place before she was three, as we knew it would entitle her to essential resources and support, without which she wouldn't be able to survive in mainstream school. Because of her summer birthday, Lubna started school very early, at the tender age of four-and-a-half, and was one of the youngest children in her class. Not only was she the youngest, she was also extremely small for her age. She had been in nappies till quite late, as we let her choose her own moment to leave them behind, and she still had a dummy at night (and at moments of high stress) for most of the time she was in the infants.

'Lubna, what did you have for dinner today?' Gail watches Lubna devour a banana, an apple and three biscuits in rapid succession on her return from school. Lubna tilts her head and stares into space thoughtfully for some minutes.

'I think it was brown.'

'Was it a pie?'

'What's a pie?'

'OK. Did you chew it, or was it like a drink?'

'I chewed it.'

'Was there any potato, or anything green?' Lubna shakes her head.

'Did you like it?'

'No. I didn't eat it.'

'So why did you choose it?'

'They put it on my plate. Grace had chips. I didn't get any chips.' She looks sad.

'Yes, but, sweetheart, you can choose. You just have to tell the dinner ladies what you want.'

'But I can't see.'

It turns out that she is so small she can't see over the rims of the trays of food at the serving hatch and has been randomly nodding at anything suggested to her. The teacher for the deaf goes into dinner with her the next day and asks the dinner staff to tilt the trays towards her so she can see what she's choosing. There are many more similar misunderstandings along the way as she stumbles through the bewildering obstacle course of the school day.

Because of her statement, Lubna has been able to go to a nursery, a primary school and a secondary school that have a unit for hearing impaired children. In her lessons the teachers wear a radio aid, which broadcasts their voices directly into her hearing aid. She also gets a support teacher in some lessons, and for a few hours each week she is withdrawn from the classroom to have sessions in the unit with the teacher for the deaf and specialist support staff. In time, her statement has expanded to include not just help for her hearing impairment but also help for a learning difficulty called auditory processing disorder, which means she has problems processing information from her short-term memory into her long-term memory. She learnt the letters of the alphabet and forgot them again many times over until she finally learnt to read at the age of eight. And she only arrived at that monumental achievement through painstaking work on the part of the teacher for the deaf, using concrete tactile forms to help her learn the letters through her body rather than her mind. In contrast, she learnt to read music (that most abstract of forms) instantly, when she took up the clarinet, as the rising and falling sounds she was making with her breath and lips matched the rising and falling notes she was following with her eyes on the page.

Being deaf has always been central to Lubna's identity, and is probably the most significant factor at school as it affects everything she does in the classroom. She is positive about being deaf and keen for people to know about her hearing aids and her auditory processing disorder, which she used to call her "memory problem" and is now learning to call by its full title. She usually wears her hair tied back so people can see her hearing aids and will understand if they need to repeat what they say, and she is starting to become aware of being part of the deaf community. The deaf children in her nursery, primary and secondary schools have their own positive place as a little family within the school. Being deaf gives them a shared experience that bridges the usual gulfs between different age groups in the school. The children in the hearing impaired unit at the secondary school watch out for the younger ones as they come up from primary school. Lubna and another girl with hearing aids in her class have been through their whole school lives together since they were in the nursery unit at three years old and, although they are not close friends, they feel an inevitable solidarity.

More recently, we have helped Lubna develop her deaf identity by asking for her to be taught how to sign. This was discouraged when she was younger as it was thought to be either unnecessary or distracting for children who could hear with aids, to learn sign language. But when a deaf children's youth club was set up locally, Lubna realised how isolated she was from all the profoundly deaf children in our area, who go to a different secondary school, with a different unit where their first language is British Sign Language. She also needs to be able to sign as she is an able swimmer and swims for the British deaf swimming team. Everyone else in the team can sign and the coaches conduct their training sessions in British Sign Language, so it has become urgent for Lubna to learn. Thankfully, she has had some intensive tuition from the Hearing Impaired Service at home and at school, and I have also been on a British Sign Language course at college so I can learn alongside her.

Lubna is a swimmer. She took to swimming from when

she was a toddler, going to a local parent and toddler session called "Aquababes" at our local swimming pool. By the age of nine, she had kicked and splashed her way through all the levels of the swimming lesson programme and was ready to join a swimming club and start training for competitions. Learning to swim without her hearing aids meant she had to rely heavily on lip reading the coach's instructions and getting her cues about what was required of her from other children. She was lucky that her first coach was a very understanding woman who always checked that Lubna understood the instructions for her lane and would give Lubna individual instructions if there was any doubt. She made steady progress in the club, both in her swimming and socially. Making friends outside school in an environment where she initially knew no one, and most of the time can't hear what's going on, has been a huge personal achievement for her and I really take my hat off to her. Recently, she swam for the national team in the European Deaf Swimming Championships in Germany. Participating in an environment where most people's first language is British Sign Language has increased her confidence as a deaf person.

As with every other essential strand in the tapestry of our lives, we have always talked about the children's birth and foster families as part of the collective history of our whole family, and we have actively promoted any direct or indirect contact that was possible. We took Maya back to London once or twice a year in the first few years she was with us, to see her foster family. These visits were quite awkward and eventually stopped after an occasion when Mrs Greaves wasn't there, though the arrangement had been made a long time in advance. On our own initiative, we enabled Maya to visit Rani in India every two or three years and, while there, to see her birth father and grandfather.

Lubna places great emphasis on her relationships with

her birth and foster families and includes all members of both, and all members of Gail's and my extended families, in her definition of her own extended family. When she was placed, we asked to meet both her birth parents before the adoption went to court. We felt that it was important for us to be able to say to Lubna that we had met Joanne and Sajid, and to be able to describe them to her. However, it wasn't easy to organise. Joanne and Sajid had both been quite negative about their daughter being placed with lesbians and neither was in a good place in their life at that time. Joanne's mother was more positive about us as she had lesbian friends herself and the plan picked up when she offered to accompany her daughter to meet us. The meeting that took place was extremely emotional for all of us. Joanne sat with her head down, her hair obscuring her eyes. Her small, girlish figure looked very fragile in a thin white sleeveless top in the middle of winter.

'Will you tell her I didn't want to give her up?' Joanne asks, her voice thick and indistinct. She has the same hearing loss as Lubna, but hearing aid technology for children was not well developed when she was a child and her hearing aids may have been more of a hindrance than a help. She didn't wear them, out of shame and embarrassment, and has not learnt to speak clearly.

'Of course we will.'

'Now I've met you, I'm glad she's going to be with you.' She struggles to continue through her welling emotions. 'I do love her.'

'We'll tell her.'

'If Sajid hadn't gone to prison just when she was born I might have been alright, but without him to help me…'

Sajid acknowledges this too, when we visit him in prison. He missed the birth of his daughter when he was first locked up and more recently he has also missed his father's funeral. A tall, gaunt, dark-skinned man with brooding eyes, he is distraught about his absence from both events and his voice is heavy with bitterness.

'I don't want her to be adopted, but I'm stuck in here now, there's nothing I can do. I don't blame Joanne, I knew she wouldn't be able to manage without me.' He is frank, and oddly friendly, about his opposition to us adopting Lubna. 'I don't agree with how you two live, but I can see you're good people. I appreciate you coming in here to see me like this.'

Once these visits are over, our contact with Joanne and Sajid is confined to the annual "letterbox" contact ordered by the court at the adoption hearing. Every year, we send school photos and information about Lubna's progress to the department that organises letterbox contact for adopters and birth families in Lubna's adoption agency. For some years we didn't get anything back, but eventually, once Sajid was out of jail and back with Joanne, we received some photos of them with their cat, and a letter saying how much they missed Lubna and thought about her, and telling her that Joanne had converted to Islam and had a Muslim name now as well as her English name.

When Lubna was ten, Marcia, the social worker who had helped us find a third child, rang us to say she had been involved in placing another child and had realised, as she uncovered the details of the child's birth family, that he was in fact Lubna's younger brother. He had been alive for three years without us knowing anything about him. He had been on the "At Risk" register when Joanne was pregnant with him, as Lubna had been, but he had been left at home when he was born, as it was felt that Joanne was coping, with support from Sajid. At the point when we found out about him he was nearly four, had been taken into care, and his development was seriously delayed. He could not talk and had quite limited understanding and ability to relate to others. Lubna was really excited to find out about his existence. She has always placed huge importance on any news of her birth family and regards them as central to her life.

We kept our promise to Lauren and Patrick to keep in touch, and have visited them most years, which has become more complicated as they are no longer together. We visited them both this summer and discovered to our astonishment that their eldest son, Kieran, who was most hostile to us when Lubna was placed, has been out as a gay man for some years and has been living with his partner for five years now. It may be that Kieran's teenage threats to kidnap Lubna were so violent because our lesbian relationship struck too close to home for him.

Of the three children, Saira has been the least interested in her birth family. As the youngest, she seems to get all the affirmation she needs from her two older sisters and her two mothers and expresses little need for any kind of family ties beyond our household. We see her former foster carers, Pat and Dave, at least once a year. Saira enjoys visiting them and seems to feel a real connection with them, but whereas Lubna was thinking about her birth mother, and worrying about her, as soon as she could talk, Saira shows limited interest in anyone beyond Pat and Dave and almost never asks anything about her birth mother, Lisa. We met Lisa once: she was very positive about us, having chosen us herself. She seemed quite low about her relationship with Saira's father, Arif, and hinted that one day soon she might need to "disappear". She has never sent any communications for Saira's letterbox contact and the social workers have never been able to pass any of our communications on to her. Saira doesn't talk about this resounding silence, so it's hard to gauge the impact on her. If she talks about her birth parents at all, she seems more interested in her birth father – maybe because she has a plethora of mothers and potential mother figures in her life, but no father figure, and she has a faint, nagging sense of a gap there. One Father's Day, she spent ages making a card, which we kept, but are not able to pass on as her birth father did not want to be contacted. He is a mysterious and totally absent figure, the only birth parent of the three sets of birth parents whom we were not able to arrange a meeting with at any point.

'You know when I was in Year 1?' Saira broaches, out of the blue, as the four of us are walking along the South Bank on a weekend in London for a friend's sixtieth birthday party. Maya lives and works in Scotland now, so if there are four of us it is usually Gail, Lubna, Saira and me.

'Ye-es.' I lean my ear slightly towards her. I hardly need to lean down any more, Saira is nearly as tall as me at ten years old. In fact they are all three almost the same height at present, as Lubna and Saira, with their towering Pathan birth fathers, ease into gear to overtake dark, diminutive South Indian Maya. Our prediction is that when they are all adults, their heights will go in reverse order to their ages and Lubna will remain, as always, in the middle.

'I said my dad was in the army.'

'The army! Why did you do that?'

'I don't know. I think they were all talking about their dads and I wanted to have something to say, so I lied. I said he was in the army and he had lots of guns and stuff and I'd ask him if I could bring them in to show everyone.'

'So what did the teacher say?'

'It was just Alex and Jack on my table, the teacher wasn't there. But I was a bit worried about having to bring something in.'

'And you didn't tell anyone?'

'No, 'cause I'd lied.' I give her a quick hug.

'You silly sausage, you should tell us when you're worried. So, do you mind not having a dad?'

'Sometimes...But I don't want one.'

'Why?'

'They're messy.'

I have an image in my mind of Saira, as a toddler, clambering all over a male friend as he lies on the floor playing dead. I suddenly see how Saira is enjoying the rough and tumble with a father figure. She enjoys some of that boisterous play with us too, piggy backs, carrying her on my shoulders, chasing, skipping, so I don't think it's a huge gap, but the absence of a father does matter to her, whereas it means nothing to Maya and is of fairly minimal significance to Lubna.

When I asked Maya, Lubna and Saira what was the most important thing about them, they each revealed different priorities. For Maya, being a woman was paramount; for Lubna being deaf and being dual-heritage were equal firsts; and Saira chose being adopted out of the choices I gave her, and insisted on adding a priority of her own that took precedence over all of my suggestions, which was "being a human bean"!

Maya has been deeply involved in left-wing politics since school, and at the age of sixteen led a walkout of students from her school to join a citywide young people's demonstration against the threatened declaration of war on Iraq. She has been active in campaigns against global capitalism, for the rights of various oppressed minorities, and in women's campaigns for abortion rights and against domestic and sexual violence. Her political activities at university are uncannily reminiscent of my own and Gail's student careers spent in the Anti-Nazi League, the Campaign for Nuclear Disarmament, Anti-Apartheid, and the women's peace movement. She is so much her two mothers' daughter!

Maya always refers to us as "my parents", rather than "my mums" and often has to correct a resulting assumption of heterosexuality, which she takes in her stride. When I asked her how she talks about us, and our family, to other people, her first response was, 'I don't'. She explained that she is rarely in a situation where she has to present information about her family cold – usually, bits of the picture filter through over time as she gets to know people. Occasionally, she takes a particular delight in wrong-footing people who have not yet been fully briefed.

The day after the "Stop the War" walkout at school, Maya was called in to see a senior teacher about her unruly and subversive behaviour. The discussion between them became heated and Mrs Kent threatened to play her trump card, usually very effective with children from middle-class backgrounds like Maya.

'I will not tolerate such rudeness, Maya. I am going to ring your mother.'

'Fine!' Maya flashed back triumphantly, 'Which one?'

More recently, we were visiting Maya in her flat in Scotland and a new flatmate came home from work while we were there. She had only been in the flat a few days. She didn't know anyone very well but she did know that Maya's family was coming up from England that day.

'Hello!' She breezed into the room loudly and cheerfully. 'Which one of you is Maya's mum, then?'

'We both are.' Gail's smile was nothing if not pleasant. Lorna's face flushed with horror.

'Oh my God!' She covered her flaming cheeks. 'I am SO sorry! I don't know why I said that, I feel so stupid!'

In response to my question about how she describes her family, Lubna wrote:

> *I have two mums, two sisters, two grandparents, three foster brothers, one foster mum, one foster dad, one birth mum, one birth dad and one birth brother. If I was interviewed and they said to me, 'How would you describe yourself?' I would say, 'I'm dual-heritage, I'm adopted and I'm deaf. I think they're the most important things to me!' If someone said to me, 'Who's picking you up from school?' I would say, 'My mum,' if I didn't know them very well. If I did know them, I would say 'Ruby', or 'Gail'. I think my adoptive family and my foster family are my families.*

In describing her family, Saira places particular emphasis on being adopted and having sisters who are also adopted. The fact that her mothers are lesbians doesn't feature at all. Her place as the youngest in the family seems to matter a lot in defining who she is. She wrote about this:

> *I have 2 sistus and 2 mums. I live with my granmar and grampar. I was adopted when I was just a babey, and so are my 2 sistus. I am the youngest and I am 10. My 2 sistus are 24 and 14.*

14

Three sisters; two mothers

It is now eighteen years since we began this journey and fifteen years since Maya began transforming our lives. When I stop and think about it, the path we have followed is still miraculous to me. Most of the time we are too busy living it to notice, and it is still unfolding.

7.15am: The special vibrating alarm clock social services supplied her with goes off under Lubna's pillow. She is immediately catapulted from her deep, silent sleep into a state of focused alertness. Every morning she turns out like this with military precision: organises herself, feeds the rabbit, Flopsy (whose much-mourned companion, Topsy, lies buried beneath the cherry tree), puts crusts out for the birds, brings in the milk from the doorstep for us, and for her grandparents, and even has time for a few words with them while the rest of us are too busy matching odd socks and hunting for hairbrushes to stop and chat. It takes many rousings to stir Saira from her bed but, despite leaving it till the last possible moment, she usually manages to be at the door beside her sister when it is time to go.

8.15am: The twin girls next door, who are the same age as Saira, emerge from their front door as we do, blowing clouds of vapour into the freezing air. They and the two boys across the road have gone to different primary schools, but they will all end up with Lubna and Saira in the same comprehensive. The girls are from one of the few white English families in the street. The boys' mother is Pakistani dual-heritage and her white husband was brought up in India. Directly opposite us lives Peter, who is Malaysian dual-heritage, and has a Polish girlfriend and an Australian lodger, while our other immediate neighbour is African-Caribbean, and further up and down the road are quite a number of Pakistani and Bangladeshi families. For Lubna and Saira, this is all they have known and it is what they imagine all English streets and communities to be like. Last year my father went into hospital while we were on a fortnight's holiday in Scotland, and my sister was amazed at how the neighbours rallied round. Now Peter, from across the road, has morning coffee regularly with my parents, and visits them every day when we are away to fetch the paper and check if they need anything. The warmth and support our neighbours offer has been important in showing the children that we are able to live our lives openly, and that we belong in our local community.

We wave the twins off down the street as Lubna and Saira jostle for the best position from which to scrape thick ice off our windscreen. They have an intense, and sometimes stormy, sibling relationship and seem closer in age than the four years that separate them. Saira is able to match Lubna in many activities and, at fourteen, Lubna is lucky to be able to return to the imaginative play of childhood with a younger sibling. On holiday, they play together with total commitment in their own worlds of cheetahs, puppies and mythical creatures. They also have violent conflicts on a regular basis; they argue over the smallest things; and no point is too tiny to become a trophy to be fought over, whether it be the chair they sit on at dinner or the number of peas on the plate! They miss each other hugely if they spend any time apart. When Lubna is away at swimming galas or sleepovers, Saira refuses all sorts of treats, such as going to the cinema or the park.

'I don't want to go without Lubna,' she will say. 'Can I just stay at home?'

8.20am: The windscreen cleared, Lubna and Saira tumble into the car. Maya was able to walk to both her primary and secondary schools, but Lubna's statement for hearing impairment has put her in a school that is a mile-and-a-half away. Saira has followed her into the same school, so we take them both in the car each day. Gail is taking them this morning. While she was still teaching, Gail acquired a studio in a city centre art space and after twenty years' service in our local comprehensive, she has recently been studying art at university. This has meant she is more available in the week to be around for the children and my parents. I work most of the week, but my part-time hours still allow me to drop the children off and pick them up two days each week. We make sure both of us are seen regularly at the school gate, just as we did fifteen years ago when Maya was at primary school. We have been visible from the beginning and spend a lot of time chatting to other parents and engaging with the staff. We have never encountered any hostility and have assumed that anyone who has a problem with us just avoids us, as there is no way they can be under any illusions about our relationship. Gail recalls that early on in Saira's first term in reception, she was collecting her in the playground at the end of the day when a boy from the same class came running up to Saira and asked,

'Is it true you have two mums?'

'Yes.'

'OK!' the child shrugged, and ran off again, having apparently settled the matter in his mind.

8.30am: After fetching the morning paper for my

parents, I take my father's car to work. In the last few years he has slowly given up driving, as his Parkinson's disease has increasingly affected his mobility, and we use the car to help us fit in all the things we need to do for them and ourselves. I leave them listening to Radio 4, promising to be back in good time to take my father to a consultant's appointment at the hospital this afternoon. I also need to pick up the children as Gail has a seminar timetabled, frustratingly, from three till five. Universities seem to take no account of the school day, even on a Master's course full of mature part-time students. Fortunately, today is Saira's netball practice, so I won't have to pick them up till half past four. On other days she does cross-country and athletics after school. Our younger two children are bewilderingly sporty given that Gail, Maya and I have never shown interest in anything more athletic than cycling to work, hill-walking, and the occasional swim.

9.30am: At my desk in the offices of Amal Black Women's Refuge, I am gathering up materials for a training session with the women in the refuge due to start at ten, when I get a frantic text from Lubna saying she has forgotten a form with her exam number for her Science GCSE test this afternoon, which she pinned on the cork noticeboard by the phone last night. I text her back to say, 'Don't panic! Will bring paper to school reception at 12.45 b4 take Grandpa to hosp.'

10.00am: My training session is, as usual, unruly. I support women who are learning the alphabet alongside others who have degrees from abroad and write textbook English in ornate longhand. I barely draw breath for two hours and watch the clock desperately at the end as we negotiate whether or not to have a session next week. It will be Eid-ul-Adha at some point, but no one knows which day, as different branches of Islam will celebrate on different days and the women are waiting for word from their respective mosques. In the end, we leave it that I will be here anyway and they will let me know nearer the time.

1.00pm: Lubna's paper successfully delivered to school, my father and I set off for the hospital. The day is clear and crisp, and he is struck by the rich autumn colours on the trees lining the way. I feel guilty that I have so little time to take them out and make a mental note to ask my sister if she can take them for a drive in the half-term holiday while we are visiting Maya in Scotland.

My father monitors his symptoms closely himself and always takes a full report to his appointments. He speaks for himself and the doctor is patient with the slowness of his speech. A couple more decades and this might be me, I think, and wonder which of our daughters, if any, might lend us a hand. My parents never expected me to stick around for them and it was that very lightness of touch and absence of expectation that made it possible to contemplate joining our lives to theirs so intimately. I have no expectations of Maya, Lubna and Saira – I only hope they will stay in touch with us. Our experience with Maya is of a continuing closeness, affection and mutual understanding that has strengthened in the five years since she first went away. Saira is adamant she will never leave home. She cannot remember not being with us, but she clings to us as if haunted by the memory that she was once somewhere else and could be whisked away again. She is a stay-at-home girl and just wants her mums.

2.30pm: We leave a prescription to be processed at the hospital pharmacy and I drop my father off at home and return to work to clear the tea trays and other debris from my training room and catch up with colleagues and paperwork.

4.30pm: I arrive in the school hall to find netball still in progress. How tall Saira is next to the other girls! It seems only a couple of years ago I was carrying her into the playground in a baby's car seat to pick Lubna up from the infants. When the final whistle blows, my new extra-leggy

Saira skips across the hall to greet me, sweaty and triumphant.

'I'm picked for the match!'

'Well done, you clever thing! When is it?'

'I think it's next week. Miss Tucker says it's in school time and we have to go to another school. She wants our parents to take us...'

'Oh, great! Well, I'll talk to Lucy's mum...' They are mostly "somebody's mum" rather than themselves, the other mums. I wonder if we are just "Saira's mums", and how they differentiate between us. Better not go there. 'Go and get changed. Lubna'll be here in a minute.' Lubna has been hanging out at her friend's house since the end of her school day and should be walking down the hill to meet us.

'All my friends can't believe Lubna's going to college already!' Saira informs me as we walk out of the school. Lubna has started a vocational course in Animal Care at college one day a week, at a site sixteen miles away, where she doesn't know anyone. 'Mrs Ward's really proud of her.'

'How did she know?' I am puzzled.

'I told her.' I stop and turn to her, smiling in amazement.

'Have you been telling everyone about Lubna's Animal Care? That's so sweet!'

I forget sometimes how much Saira looks up to Lubna and how proud they are of each other.

5.15pm: We travel home via the hospital pharmacy to pick up the prescription dropped off earlier and by the time we get home they are both desperately hungry. We have missed afternoon tea with their grandparents, so I supply fruit and snacks to keep them going and try to think, not very creatively, about dinner. Gail and I try to avoid having fixed roles in the house, but cooking is one area where we have a very clear division of labour. Gail enjoys it and I have inherited a deep insecurity about it from my mother, who was never taught to cook, as the youngest of nine in an

Indian household with a resident cook. She learnt to cook when she came to England from *Mrs Beeton's Book of Household Management* and other similar tomes, but never developed any confidence and her enduring anxiety in the kitchen has transferred itself to me. Friends arriving for dinner and seeing bowls of succulent curries, *dhal*, rice and chapattis might be forgiven for attributing the spread to me. In fact, I rarely do more than boil pasta or grill fish fingers. When Maya is home, Gail gets to talk cooking with someone who loves creating food as much as she does, and we are treated to a succession of gastronomic delights. When neither of them is around, Lubna and Saira are happy to eat pot noodles and pizza.

Today I decide to make an effort, and start chopping onions and vegetables for a pasta sauce. When the sauce is simmering respectably, I go in search of Lubna, who is watching *Eastenders* on playback on the one computer we all share, while flicking through texts on her mobile phone. Gail and I will not have televisions or computers in bedrooms, or any kind of electronic games in the house. Maya never wanted such things and didn't have a mobile phone until she was sixteen, but we are aware that Lubna and Saira are almost of a different generation and their peer groups have grown up with technology literally at their fingertips, at all times. They complain sometimes about how deprived they are in this area, but they also spend all year looking forward, like we do, to our fortnight by the sea in the house without electricity or mobile phone signal. I'm glad they can use their imaginations, and cardboard boxes, to play.

I want Lubna to do some Animal Care homework while the pasta sauce is cooking, but she claims she "needs" to text her best friend about a drama involving a boy that will unravel before our eyes unless she lends immediate moral support. Her persistence is exhausting. All three of our daughters can argue for England and accept no authority as self-evident. This is largely thanks to Gail and her feisty, if random, upbringing, with all its rough edges and early training in fighting your corner. Mine was a much more polite, inhibited, afternoon-tea-and-Bridge-after-dinner kind of upbringing, imported from an India of the 1930s and reinforced by my father's working life in academia. While recognising in principle the huge value for girls in growing up being able to say "no" without guilt or hesitation, I struggle in practice with the failure of our children to defer to me automatically as an "elder and better".

'Do the homework first, and then you can text whoever you like,' I insist.

She follows me grumpily back to the kitchen and we pore over listings outlining the markings and characteristics of seventy varieties of snakes, trying to identify the ones pictured on the homework sheet. We had a two-month battle last summer to get Lubna onto this Animal Care course, which she attends one day a week in place of three GCSE subjects. Looking after animals is all she has ever wanted to do, from being a toddler, and this course gives her a weekly release from the pressures of more academic subjects which threaten to totally demoralise her. Gail and I field different battles at different times when it comes to advocating for our children. I did the Animal Care campaign, while Gail is currently lobbying the school about Information Technology, which has become too abstract and theoretical for Lubna. Like hosts of other parents of children with additional learning needs across the country, we spend large proportions of our time dealing with unwieldy and unresponsive institutions, making ourselves the bane of some middle manager's life and learning to live with that because our children matter more than being squeamish about "bothering" the professionals or being labelled "pushy".

6.00pm: Gail arrives home and I serve up the pasta and

vegetable sauce, which is wolfed down virtually without complaint, except from Saira, who wants noodles at every meal. After dinner, we ring Maya to make arrangements for our visit at half-term. Lubna tells her about Animal Care and going rollerskating with her friend, Ali, at the weekend. Ali is coming out as gay at the age of fourteen and he confides all his problems to Lubna, who is happy to support him.

'Ali's from Yemen,' I hear her telling Maya. 'His family are Muslim but he says he's page or something – yes, pagan! He's like me because he's kind of Asian, but he's different from other Asian people because he's gay and he's not a Muslim...We get on really well...I know, but I like him.' Maya must have spotted the wistfulness in her tone.

Saira wants to talk to Maya too, but is monosyllabic when she gets on the phone, lost for words before the disembodied voice of her big sister. Maya represents all that her younger sisters aspire to in hair, make-up, clothes, music and lifestyle. They are slightly in awe of her dazzling poise and presence and her disapproval carries far more weight than our all too familiar reprimands. Because she has been away for most of the last five years, on a gap year in India and a four-year degree course in Scotland, her time and attention are hugely treasured and sometimes fought over, and her strict ideological positions on things like ethical shopping, healthy eating and television viewing choices have a direct impact on her sisters' behaviour.

Maya and Gail plan a trip to an art exhibition when we visit, and discuss the all-important matter of where and when we will eat on the Saturday night, as some television chef has just opened a new restaurant near her that is proving a huge success. We might just get a table if we are prepared to eat at five in the afternoon, and then we can go back to the flat and watch Maya and her flatmates dressing up to go out to a Hallowe'en Burlesque Night at their local club, a spectacle that will enthral Lubna and Saira, even though they will be going to bed when the young women teeter out to a taxi at ten o'clock at night, in driving Highland rain. Maya will return at four in the morning and get up again at eight to serve breakfasts in the bistro where she works near her flat. On top of working to pay the bills, she has applied to volunteer in local women's refuges and with projects supporting asylum seekers. She is thinking about training in social work and is trying not to worry about levels of graduate unemployment. I know she has the skills and maturity to do the work, and I also know the emotional costs and burnout endemic in the field.

'When you come up, can we spend some time on my interview for the Women's Aid volunteer placement?' she asks me when the phone is passed to me.

'Of course. I'm sure you'll be fine, they should be biting your hand off.'

'It doesn't feel like that. It's taken them weeks to get back to me. At this rate I won't start anything till after Christmas, and then how will I fit in going to India before it gets too hot there?'

'Have you asked your boss about Christmas yet?'

'Yes, he was fine about it. I'm coming home on the nineteenth for ten days and then coming back up here for New Year.'

'Fantastic! I'm quite looking forward to Christmas now!'

The prospect of Maya being around in the lead-up to Christmas transforms it for me from a chore, and the unattractive orgy of consumerism that it is, into a delightful battening down of the hatches against winter storms, curling up on the settee before a good film with coffee and mince pies, and a real celebration of what makes us a family. Maya has a talent for occasions. When she first arrived, she was passionate about family rituals and traditions, creating many of them herself, and now she lives away from home for most of the year, Christmas is more precious than ever to her. She seems able to hold a much more sophisticated balance between challenging the status quo and valuing the social cement of ritual, than the wholesale scorn I held for tradition when I was her age.

'How are things in Essex? Is Boxing Day still happening?' Maya catches my silent hesitation.

'Oh, yes, there'll always be Boxing Day, but it's not easy, is it? I think everyone's coping and it will be lovely to see all the new babies.'

Christmas has been a particularly difficult time for Gail and her siblings since Gail's parents and her sister's four-year-old granddaughter died within a few months of each other in one year. Her father died in the May after a long, known illness; four-year-old Kylie died of cancer in early December; and Gail's mother died very unexpectedly at Christmas. The following Christmases, we could barely drag ourselves through the preparations. Gail was expending a lot of emotional energy producing artwork on her degree course linked to the deaths, and I was working with trauma in two challenging part-time counselling jobs and not admitting to myself how overstretched I was feeling. One year we sent virtually no Christmas cards and it was a huge effort to think about presents and decorations. That year, Maya asked if her friend, Devi, could come to us for Christmas. We had visited Maya and Devi in India when they were on their gap year and had told Devi then that she was welcome to spend her Christmases with us, as her parents were returning to India after more than three decades in Britain. When it came to it, I wasn't sure we were up to having a guest in the house.

Maya and Devi arrived a couple of days before Christmas, bearing gifts and smiles. An extraordinary lightness, like sunshine, floated in with them. Coming from a Hindu family, Devi had never experienced Christmas before and found everything enchanting. They helped Lubna and Saira wrap their presents, played games with them, decorated the Christmas tree, and Maya helped Gail cook the Christmas dinner, while Devi and I laid the table downstairs with crackers, candles and my parents' best linen and crockery. After dinner we sang carols, with Devi accompanying on Lubna's clarinet, Maya on the recorder, and my father on the piano. The happiness on Lubna and Saira's faces, because they were making music with the big girls, the warmth and affection in the room, and my awareness of the fragility of it all, choked me so that I could hardly sing.

'I need to go and cook some dinner now. Can I email you the person spec for the Women's Aid thing?'

'Yep. I'll make sure I read it before we come. And see you then?'

'Yes, thanks. See you then!'

7.00pm: Lubna and I drive to the leisure centre for her swimming training. While she is getting changed, I buy a coffee in the canteen before it shuts and find a seat in the viewing gallery over the swimming pool. I have spent many hours of my life in this leisure centre, watching training sessions and swimming galas, and I am heartily sick of its machine-brewed coffees and vacuum-packed caramel shortbreads. The atmosphere in the pool area is hot and steamy as a sauna and I peel off my winter layers as I settle down near the other parents. Sometimes I sit and chat, at other times I sit at a distance and write, or work on my laptop. No one minds; we accept each other's strategies for surviving the penance of spending our lives in swimming pools, as other parents do on football fields, in dance studios and scout halls, and all manner of inhospitable venues up and down the country. There are a significant number of black swimmers and their families in the swimming club and there is one other disabled swimmer who swims in all the disability galas with Lubna, but we are the only lesbian or gay parents in the club. As with school, we don't really know what everyone else thinks of us, but we have met only openness and warmth, and Lubna receives endless encouragement and support from her friends in the club.

9.30pm: Lubna and I return home after an hour-and-a-half of training. While she hangs her swimsuit and towel to dry over a radiator, I pop into Saira's room to say goodnight, as Gail put her to bed over an hour ago. Saira is sitting up listening to a story tape and cutting out shapes from sheets of coloured paper. She whips the scissors under her bedclothes guiltily as I burst into the room.

'Too late! Why are you still up doing things? You should be lying down nice and snug so you can fall asleep. Look at the time!'

'I'm waiting for Lubna.' She hates going to sleep without Lubna securely ensconced in the next room.

'Well, she's here now so you can lie down. Come on, give me the scissors.' I place her shapes and scissors carefully on the desk and she hugs me tightly before snuggling down into her covers and turning off her light.

'Goodnight-love-you-see-you-in-the-morning,' she calls her nightly refrain as I leave and I reply with the same words. She will be asleep long before the tape ends.

Lubna passes me as I emerge from Saira's room and mumbles her own exhausted goodnight.

'Good swimming tonight, well done.' I kiss her lowered head, her preferred daily gesture of affection. 'See you in the morning.'

The ten o'clock news has started before Gail and I settle down in the front room and get our first opportunity to catch up with each other.

'We've got a new assignment. I have to write my life in bullet points on one side of A4,' she tells me, stretching out on her crimson settee. I pile up the cushions on mine and sink back into them with my mug of coffee. The heating is going off now and we would be warmer if we closed the curtains, but I like the deep indigo of the night sky above the rooftops opposite, and the twinkle of streetlights across the valley. As my parents live on the ground floor, our front room is high above the stone bay and looks out over the back gardens of an adjacent street to the same circle of hills we could see from our old house; we are just half a mile further up the valley. In the winter we can see the bright windows of trains hurtling along the valley bottom through the bare branches of the tree in front of our house. Sometimes in the early hours we hear an owl hooting loudly outside our attic bedroom and its partner hooting back from further away.

'Hey, I like that idea! I think I'll do it too. Maybe I could use it at work...Maya sounds well, doesn't she? I forgot to ask her if she wants us to take her anything.'

'I asked her last week and she said she wants her Afghan coat and a hot water bottle.'

'It must be freezing in that flat.'

'I think they try not to have the heating on if they can help it. Either that or it doesn't work very well.'

'Remember last year when it snowed in the middle of April?' Gail nods as we remember the dazzling white mountains of mainland Scotland suspended in mist across the Sound like a distant Himalayan range.

'What are you doing on Friday?' She glances across at me and I flick through the diary in my head. Friday is my nominal day off as I am on a part-time contract, but it doesn't always work out like that.

'I'm taking Mum to the dentist first thing, but she should be finished by eleven. Shall we go out for lunch and a bit of a walk?'

'That would be nice.' Her reply understates the extent to which quality time on our own as a couple is precious and necessary to our survival. A bracing walk on windswept moors, followed by lunch with an extensive view of russet hillsides, will expand the emotional spaces within, as well as the physical spaces without, and give us time to tease out the thornier issues of family life. There are always new thorny issues to take the place of those from which we have pulled the thorns. What has grown over the years is our confidence to weather the storms and our faith in the wisdom and resilience of our children.

'That's sorted then.'